Of this book 1,000 copies have been printed,
of which numbers 1 to 100 have been specially
bound and signed by the author of the Introduction
and the artist

THIS COPY IS NUMBER. *176* ....

ON THE MAKING OF GARDENS

SIR GEORGE SITWELL

ON
THE MAKING
OF
GARDENS

WITH AN INTRODUCTION BY
SIR OSBERT SITWELL

AND DECORATIONS BY
JOHN PIPER

THE DROPMORE PRESS

1949

TO
MY MOTHER
THIS ESSAY
IS DEDICATED

HORTUS CONCLUSUS:
MY FATHER AND THE GARDEN

IN THE HAPPY DAYS OF THE FAR-OFF FIRST
decade of the nineteen hundreds, about the
time that Princess Ena became engaged to King
Alphonso, that Melba was first singing in *Madame
Butterfly*, that Miss Lily Elsie was appearing in *The
Merry Widow*, in short, in the golden days of good
King Edward, a visitor in the spring or autumn to
any of the great Italian or remarkable Sicilian gardens, especially those that were more remote, might
have chanced to see a tall, distinguished-looking
Englishman with a high-bridged nose, and with
fair, fine hair and a slightly darker golden moustache,
flourished upwards a little in the manner of the
Kaiser, seated on a bench, regarding his surround-

i

ings with analytic attention. Probably he would be sitting on an air-cushion, and would be wearing a grey suit and a wide, grey hat, while beside him—for he was careful to sit in the shade—was a sun-umbrella lined with green. Not far off, within the carrying of a voice, from the thick blackness of an ilex grove would peer a ponderous figure, watchful, but with an eye for those who passed as well as for the safety of the square, varnished wicker box in his care; which each day contained a cold chicken. As he stood there he had something of an air of a night watch on a ship, and his appearance, though his skin was bronzed, or indeed copper-coloured, was as northern and national as that of the gentleman on the bench. He, meanwhile had taken an envelope out of his pocket and was scratching on it with the stub-end of a pencil, angry or meditative remarks; crossly, how a gardener had removed the patine of lichen from a stone moulding since last he was here, or reflectively, comparing the merits where an effect of mystery was desired of broad shaded ilex with thin spired cypress, or of the various hues, textures, and sounds of varying kinds and speeds of falling water, and the sense of coolness and peace these induced . . .

The visitors might perhaps enquire—as often they did when they got back to the hotel—who the

English gentleman might be, and the nautical figure hovering so heavily in the background—and the answer would be, Sir George Reresby Sitwell and his servant, Henry Moat. For, in those years, my father was busy collecting material for the book he planned.

In 1900, he had suffered a bad nervous breakdown and had decided in consequence to give up politics. In the ensuing years he travelled much in Italy, and of his recovery there, this book was the fruit. He had already written several works of an historical nature, or illustrative of the manners of some particular period, but had issued them from his own printing-press. They had not been for sale. But this new volume was to be published by Murray's: and its aim was high, for I recollect him saying to me that he hoped it would rank in the future, with Bacon's essay on gardens.

On the Making of Gardens certainly stands as the most complete expression in my father's writings of one facet of his personality, of one concentration of his interests—but there were hundreds of others. Though he worked so hard at all the innumerable matters on which he was engaged, the truth is that he found it difficult to finish anything. The garden at Renishaw remains—and is now likely to remain —uncompleted in its detail. And the family-history at which he had worked for two decades, was found after his death with still one chapter lacking.

Time seems to have been too short for him in his eighty-three years, and only this one book which follows is an idea of his conceived, attempted, and achieved—whatever may be judged of the achievement—wholly realised down to the last comma and the final full-stop. Moreover, when setting himself to anything, no pain was spared, either to himself or to others—it would often have been, in result, better if it had. Thus, before beginning to write this book, he spent endless hours mastering the full intricacies of English grammar, under the tuition of Major Viburne, who appears a fitful—in every sense—shadow in the pages of my autobiography, and who knew much less about it than his pupil. In fact, my father took too much trouble. To write a sentence on the psychology of garden-making, he would read a hundred slightly obsolete technical volumes, nor would he always give his imagination room for its full sweep in the matter on which he was writing. He relied overmuch on notes—for one difference between the journalist and the writer, resides in this, that the first takes notes and directly transcribes from them, while the second allows—or should allow—the subject matter of his book to grow organically, like a plant, in the mind and on the paper. Thus, in illustration of what I mean, I once saw my father setting off from the door at Renishaw in a very old carriage, about eleven on a September night. As usually he went to bed at ten, I was surprised, and enquired what he was doing; "Just driving down to Eckington Church to observe the effect of moonlight on the spire" he replied with a flutter of his hand, as if conferring a favour upon the edifice; "I want it for my chapter, *Eckington Church in the Thirteenth Century* in *Tales of My Native Village.*"

Notwithstanding, never was any book more pondered upon at every stage. For hours the author would lie on his bed wrestling with each problem, and if Henry's footstep was heard in the passage, or a hotel housemaid dared to wipe and rattle surreptitiously—a favourite trick when a writer is at work—the door handle, he would dart out of bed, clearing his mosquito net as if by magic, open the door, and look out blandly, while making at the same time a humming noise which held in it—if you listened carefully—an icy cold, but terrible, menace. (Strangers, however, were apt to mistake this sound for one engendered by happiness, and in consequence, often received strange surprises).

Unfortunately then, as I have said, his energies were dissipated over a field too broad for their employment. But though he was adept at taking hold of the wrong end of a thousand sticks, yet when by chance he seized the right end, his grasp of it was remarkable, because of the intellectual power and application, as well as the learning, which he brought to his task. And here, in *On the Making of Gardens* we have a complete work containing a great deal of thought and couched in phrases often of stilted beauty, and even if the whole book from its opening "Time is a wayward traveller" down to the closing sentence which begins "Flying shafts of silvery splendour . . ." carries for us the haunting and mocking echo of Sir Austin Feverel's *The Pilgrim's Scrip*, even if fountains throughout are inclined to "plash," and the "goat-herd" figures overmuch in a landscape not untouched by Alma Tadema, still, it's none the worse for that, being a genuine period-piece, instilled with considerable imagination, influenced by the philosophies current ten years earlier, and with, not far behind each page, those crepuscular sensations made fashionable by Maeterlinck, together with a reverberation of the august, if far-fetched, rotundities of Walter Pater. Moreover—and this is where he took the *right* end of the stick—the principles he enunciated in his volumes (so my gardening friends, whose judgment I trust, tell me) are invaluable in the practical design of gardens, in the counterpoint of light and shade, and the correct employment of water as a device for variation.

In short, he knew what he was talking about, having observed, noted, and practised. His knowledge of gardens, Italian in particular—was unrivalled (several later writers have had recourse to the lists obtained from him), but not, I hasten to add, of flowers, about which, paradoxically to English ideas of the present day, no man knew or cared less, for he had early imbibed the Mediterranean conception, imposed by brightness of climate, that a garden is a place of rest and peace, and in no way intended for a display of blossoms (for that, you had "a flower garden" away from the house, and hidden). Such flowers as might be permitted, had, like all else in good taste, to be unobtrusive, not to call attention to themselves by hue or scent, but to form vague pointillist masses of colour that could never detract from the view, and to infuse into the air a general sweetness never to be identified. The pastel-shade sweet peas and stocks of nineteen hundred, love-in-the-mist, a few washed-out roses, and a reed with a kind of blue flower—these passed muster: but even they were sacrifices to my mother's insistent demands for scent and colour. "Horticulturists blossoms" were what he most detested, and to make a personal confession, I remember that as a schoolboy on holiday, when my father had been particularly disagreeable, I used always to go out in the garden to tend a rhododendron that carried a purple blossom of a peculiarly obtrusive and fiery appearance which he could see from his study window, and which greatly offended his eye although for some reason or other he never eradicated it. This I did because I had been told by someone that if you removed the dead raceme from a branch it would flower again, and more flagrantly, the following spring.

To return to the book which follows, I remember well the initial stages of its first publication, for I had never before seen galley proofs, and my father gave them to me—I was sixteen—to read, with his corrections on them (I little knew then, how those flat paper serpents were to entangle and devour my life, as if I were Laocoon), and I used to take them into a corner of the small flat in Florence which we had rented that year, to revel in the sense of importance which this new acquaintance with the technical ways of the literary world conferred upon me... Not only were these the first corrected proofs I had seen, they were, alas, also the first I ever lost! . . . Eventually, after a week of utter ignominy and disgrace, they were found in a cupboard in my room where I had placed them for safe keeping. Later in the year—for publishing was then a quicker business altogether—my father's great moment arrived, and the book came out—I think in September 1909. But, it is sad to recall, little more happened. One or two appreciative essays such as were written in those more leisurely days, appeared in the weekly papers. He, and I, waited . . . but the rest was silence. Naturally he was disappointed, and blame was distributed impartially, some of it no doubt coming to me, and a good deal being placed to my mother's account.

I remember, too, his remarking of the top binding of his book, which was concealed under an azure dust-cover, but displayed in bright colours the hardest and most stilted of garden vistas, that "Murrays have managed to contradict with it every lesson I inculcate" . . . However, he was pleased with the printing, if not with the reception. And I think, that the actual moment of the appearance of the book was most pleasant for him. He had been ill, as the reader knows, and the process of study in gardens had healed him. The publishing of his work had constituted, moreover, a declaration of independence, and an affirmation of faith. It must have brought back to him lovely sunny days spent in his own company, which he greatly enjoyed, with

Henry and the luncheon-basket discreetly within call. Sometimes he took me with him, and on these occasions he was at his most amiable. There were, as well, adventures; such as that of which I heard subsequently from Henry, though I was not myself present. My father was meditating, just before the hour when the garden was to be closed, at the very bottom of the lay-out of Villa D'Este, between the giant cypresses. He was deep in thought, when four ancient *custodi* advanced on him from the four different quarters of the compass. Immediately, concluding the old men were brigands (for he lived always a hundred years before his time), he, as Henry put it "fair biffed 'em with his umbrella. You could hear 'em squawk half a mile away!" . . . But from such escapades, for which, alone of living men, he seemed qualified, he always emerged victorious and scot-free. It was enough in those days for Henry to explain that his master was an English *Signore*.

The effect, however, on my father of the lack of success of his book, was considerable. He had, he told me, hoped to earn by it, now that his world was threatened by Lloyd George's Budget, something to leave to my brother Sacheverell. This hope was disappointed. And then there was another side to it. Many of my mother's friends, violently opposed to books in general, now regarded him as a traitor who had placed himself on the wrong side of the fence. Only the Bevy, which I have described elsewhere, sent up at his approach, hosannahs of faint artistic praise. Meanwhile, he set himself to problems that were more immediate and practical than the theories of garden design. He arranged to send me to an army-crammer's, from which I was seldom allowed to emerge—and when I did make a sortie, was seldom to be greeted with rapture. Then he had long been at work on an invention—a stick which would discharge vitriol at mad dogs and thus dispose of them. (There had been an epidemic of hydrophobia some twenty years before, but he had never as yet completed or patented his idea). To this matter he now gave his mind. In addition, he made more miscellaneous notes; *Rotherham under Cromwell, Sheffield in the Wars of the Roses, Court Formalities at Constantinople, Marriage Chests of the Middle Ages, How to Preserve Fruit, The Correct Use of Seaweed as an Article of Diet, Sacheverell Pedigrees, My Views on Democracy;* each of these, and of a thousand other subjects had a box devoted to it. These boxes were specially made for him, to contain half pages of foolscap, and were fashioned of a material the colour of an aubergine, and in texture like a skin with goose flesh . . . Indeed, in everything

xi

connected with writing, he had his own ways. His pens, as I have described elsewhere, were of a fine, scratchy variety, composed of three long nibs fitted together making them still more light and spidery in their use. For the rest, in the world of actuality, if he could not write about gardens with success, at least he could make them. He abolished small hills, created lakes, and particularly liked now to alter the levels at which full grown trees were standing. Two old yew trees in front of the dining-room windows at Renishaw were regularly heightened and lowered; a process which I then believed could have been shown to chart, like a thermometer, the temperature of his mood, and to which he always referred as "pulling and dragging." ("That oak tree needs to be pulled and dragged!") From the wooden towers constructed for the purpose in the lake and on the hill, he would measure and survey. His head throbbed with ideas, the majority of them never to be put into practice. Glass fountains, aqueducts in rubble, gigantic figures, cascades through the woods, stone boats and dragons in the water of lake and pool, blue-stencilled white cows "to give distinction to the landscape," many of these schemes, alas, remained where they were born. But they were a fine exercise for him, and a diversion. And it must be remembered that he would be occupied, too, every day in instructing all those about him in whatever was their speciality, while at the same time he was, besides, ferociously engaged in combat over his own affairs; for, as he once rather piteously remarked to me, "One has to think of *oneself a little*."

OSBERT SITWELL

July 7, 1949   Renishaw

PREFACE

TO MANY EXCELLENT PEOPLE WHO TAKE
a gloomy view of life, studies of art and
beauty seem to be but trifling; I must therefore urge as an excuse for this essay that the greater
part of it was written during a period of broken
health, when slowly recovering from the effects of
over-work. Further, I would plead that a serious purpose lies behind it, namely, that of influencing the
newly recovered art of garden design. The revival
of garden-craft is the work of English architects,
more particularly of Sedding, R. Blomfield and
F. Inigo Thomas. But still, as in the days of Fynes
Moryson, the formal garden in England falls short
of the great examples of the Italian Renaissance; it
is seldom related as it should be to the surrounding
scenery; it is often wanting in repose and nearly

always in imagination. During the last few years several sumptuous volumes have appeared illustrating the old gardens of Italy, yet except for a few hints given by Mrs Wharton in her most valuable and charming book, little or nothing has been said about principles. If the world is to make great gardens again, we must both discover and apply in the changed circumstances of modern life the principles which guided the garden-makers of the Renaissance, and must be ready to learn all that science can teach us concerning the laws of artistic presentment.

Every one who has travelled in Italy appreciates the courtesy and kindness shown by Italians to strangers of all nationalities—perhaps one would not be wrong in saying more especially to Englishmen. Since I first began in the early 'nineties to study old Italian gardens I have visited more than two hundred in all parts of the country, and I cannot sufficiently express my thanks to the owners.

GEORGE R SITWELL

May, 1909

ON THE MAKING OF GARDENS

I

TIME IS A WAYWARD TRAVELLER, WHO sometimes rides post-haste through thick and thin, sometimes loiters on the road or falls asleep in the saddle, so that, fearing he is engulfed, we are half inclined to send with ropes and lanterns to drag him out of the deep miry ways: it is therefore not surprising if now and again the events of a century are crowded into the annals of one brief lifetime. Nowhere is this headlong rush of Time more noticeable than in the sixty years which elapsed between the publication of Bacon's essay on gardens in 1625 and that of Sir William Temple in the last year of King Charles the Second. The charm of both writers will be felt by every one, yet so different is the spirit and outlook that we seem to have passed into another world. The last wave of the great Renaissance impulse spends itself and dies in Bacon: in Temple, great events often taking their rise in a garden, we have the first suggestion of a return to nature and freedom, the first whisper of rebellion, the first breath of revolution. There is another strange difference between the two essays. Bacon, while content to work within the four-square limits which sense, moderation, and experience have imposed, is pregnant in every sentence with suggestion, fancy, imagination: Sir William is a cold formalist intent on growing better peaches and nectarines than his neighbours, and has nothing to say which his best friend could describe as imaginative, unless it be his reference to a Dutch garden at the Cape of Good Hope, divided into four parts, each planted with the trees, flowers, and fruit peculiar to one quarter of the world; an idea on a par with those which have inspired so many of our modern Memorials, and not, as Sir William himself must have been aware, belonging to a very high order of imagination.

In this there is something more than the different genius of the two men, something more than the baneful influence of Versailles. The world itself has changed, the day of humanism is over, new and narrower fetters are everywhere replacing the old.

We have reached the age of the Classical Decadence, when scholarship was sinking into pedantry, when form and correctness were more than fancy or freedom and clever technique than serious intention or high endeavour, when painting, architecture, war, poetry, love, and manners had all been reduced to rules of practice and education had come to be a knowledge of restraints. It was not permissible to admire the barbarous Gothic, nor the rugged efforts of untutored nature, nor the work of the earlier poets and masters; commerce and the care of an estate were vulgar, and to think for oneself in the realm of philosophy or religion was not only, as at present, a misdemeanour, but actually a crime. Thus it was that, thought and freedom being denied, the fine gentlemen and radiant ladies whom we see upon the canvases of Watteau, Hogarth, and Longhi took to the more pardonable vices of gambling and intrigue, to exquisite trifling in porcelain and prints and jewels and enamels and miniatures; or drowned the illusions of life in a fairy world of enchanted sound. Thus it was that, hedged in on every side by formalism, they grew weary of the silvery plash of the fountain and the bass murmur of the stepped cascade, of ordered bosquet, stiff canal and sanded parterre, of groves like green chests set upon poles, of smirking nymphs and leering satyrs

3

and fine vases full of nothing. The long straight alleys seemed to them to be insipid, the evergreen hedges to be unfeeling; they hated the flower battalions which stood on parade in platoons of pinks and regiments of tulips and armies of asters, the stage scenery of box and turf and trellis which could not share in the hopes of spring or the regrets of autumn, but was dead to all the music of the year. For in the general decadence of the arts the garden too had fallen upon evil days. Unbending system had been the fault of the French, even in the time of Montaigne, who notes that the Italians "borrow an infinity of graces, not known among us, from the very irregularity of the surface"; and in the last quarter of the seventeenth century, when the sceptre of taste and fashion passed at length from proud Italy to gaudy Versailles, the evil was intensified by Le Nôtre, who stole the formulas of garden-making from Rome and Florence, but left the poetry behind.

The long-drawn-out monotony of the new style, which took no account of the genius of the place, but sought everywhere to overwhelm nature with mighty embankments and deep-dug valleys and rivers turned from their courses, with terrace heaped upon terrace, with groves of up-springing fountains and forests of well-drilled trees, was bound to provoke a reaction. But the revolution which followed is not an isolated phenomenon: with the baroque in architecture, the Chinese taste in decoration, the freer forms of musical composition, the Romantic movement in painting and literature, it is part of a world's revolt against a formalism which had become intolerable.[1] At first the English garden, the garden of nature and sentiment which Addison and Rousseau describe, must have appeared by contrast as refreshing as in these days of lawns and shrubberies a walled enclosure is to us. In the parks attached to the great houses, where oval lakes and square islands were not unknown, there was room for the new landscape art, whose great achievement has been the management of water and the grouping of trees. But as under Louis XIV the garden had encroached upon the park, so now the park swept over the garden, bringing the "one unending undulating sweep" of the bare English lawn up to the very windows of the house. With the Peace of 1762 the

[1] In 1712, when Addison, stirred by descriptions of travel in China, was proposing to introduce into the garden the "beautiful wildness of nature," Watteau was already making it the subject of his pictures. Painting in the great neglected gardens of the Luxembourg and Montmorency, he gives indeed the statues, stairways, and stately hemicycles of the old régime, but the green irregular vistas have no limit, and every trace of regularity in pathway or vegetation has disappeared. In 1717 he produced L'Embarquement pour Cythère, "the first genuine painted poem that Europe had seen since the golden days of the Venetian Renaissance"

new fashion spread like a plague over Europe, destroying everywhere the historic and harmonious setting of hall and palace and castle, scenes which the care and love of bygone centuries had hallowed, which should have been left to us to link one generation with another. In its train came follies worse than those which provoked the satire of Addison. The garden was deprived first of its boundaries and then of its flowers, sham rivers, dead trees, and broken bridges were planted in appropriate positions, while over the countryside in the neighbourhood of the great houses there broke out a dreadful eruption of Gothic temples and Anglo-Saxon keeps, Corinthian arches and Druid amphitheatres, of classic urns, Chinese pagodas and Egyptian pyramids, all with inscriptions in Greek or black-letter appealing to the eye of taste and to the tear of sensibility.

Modern writers who wish to make the best of both gardening worlds endeavour to excuse these aberrations as excesses for which the style itself must not be held responsible, but though much may be said for the simple garden, the whole theory of the natural garden is absolutely unsound. If the house requires a platform as a statue requires a pedestal, if the bold projections and broad shadows of terrace and stairway are peculiarly valuable in the foreground, if water in a small volume is ridiculous or squalid unless set off by formal masonry, if standing pools double by reflection the beauty of flowers and trees, if the contrast of vegetation and stonework is dear to the heart of every artist, why are we to sacrifice all these advantages to a sentiment which has not even the merit of being sincere? "You will observe," says the landscapist, introducing us to his ideal pleasure ground, "that here there is nothing regular, nothing artificial, no straight lines or pleached hedges or tonsured trees; only a loving and reverent study of beautiful Nature's methods and a patient attempt to reproduce her pictures: the idea is that we are in a natural glade of the forest." Quite so, we venture to remark, but what about the mown grass and the rather undecided gravel path and the scentless roses and the rich and startling masses of horticulturists' flowers and the unhappy blotches of subtropical foliage? "We must assume," he replies, "that this is a kind of grass that doesn't grow and that the gravel path is an unfortunate accident." Very well, we say again, anxious to enter into the spirit of the thing, but what about the house; is that an unfortunate accident too? It is indeed upon this point that the theory of the landscape garden goes to total shipwreck. You can't hope to persuade us that Nature built the house: why insult our understanding by pretending that Nature made the garden? The utmost extreme to which artificiality can go is the mock-natural. If this be defended on the ground that the garden is a land of illusion in which any fraud is permissible, we are bound to point out that it is a deception which fails to deceive; if on the other hand we are asked to accept it as a frank convention, what is to be thought of all this high-flown sentiment about the graceful touch of Nature? No mastery over form can save from failure a work of art animated by a faulty or defective idea. Now Hegel has pointed out in his Æsthetics that the affectation of want of purpose and contrivance, the pretence of disorder, of natural primeval solitude in an artificial scene which has been deliberately planned for human enjoyment and for social intercourse, is one of those primary discords which no ingenuity can soften or conceal, for the jarring note will be heard above all the music of the landscape. In such a scene civilised man is out of place, and even the landscape gardener who contrived it must follow the example of the ancient Britons and put on a suit of woad, if he wishes to be in harmony with the surroundings. Yet another discord in the motive is that between the house and the woodland lawn upon which it has apparently dropped from the skies: the house is at war with the landscape and the landscape with the house, each has a different tale to tell, and no natural beauty of flower or tree can relieve us from the shock of contradiction and the pain of incongruity. Curving paths cannot be right, for the Chinese themselves, with whom the landscape style began, make their paths straight, arguing that they must be due either to design or to repeated passage, that no sober man will deliberately propose to reach his destination by a series of curves, and even if the inhabitants of a house or hamlet were to get drunk in company, that it is hardly possible they should all describe precisely the same reel of intoxication. Flower-beds in stars or moons or rounded figures cannot be right: they are simply unquiet and, as Ruskin points out, straight lines are the best foil to the grace of natural curves in plant and flower. It cannot be right to endeavour to realise in a garden the compositions of the great masters of painting, for that is to sacrifice general beauty to a few selected points of view, and how is one to compose a picture with changing materials when the foreground is wandering into the middle distance, the figures and the cattle are moving on, the saplings are burgeoning into a grove? It cannot be right to crowd together in a few acres all the mood-compelling aspects of nature, the gay, the tranquil, the romantic, the picturesque,

9

the melancholy, the tragic, the terrible, the sublime; or to fill the park with abbeys and hermitages, Greek temples and Gothic castles, which are both incongruous with each other and through meanness of scale and poverty of material do not deceive but only offend. That indeed is the final outcome of the landscape garden: it appeals to many emotions but touches only one, a peculiar kind of heart-sinking which one remembers to have experienced before upon entering some Chippendale-Gothic mansion belonging to the same period of art.

Is it not time that the world should abandon these follies of the Decadence, should turn again for inspiration to the "high-walled gardens green and old" of a happier time; that it should listen at last to the prayer of the eighteenth century poet:

Again the moss-grown terraces to raise
And spread the labyrinth's perplexing maze,
Replace in even lines the ductile yew
And plant again the ancient avenue;

that it should turn its back on Kent, Capability Brown, and Horace Walpole, and should seek to learn the principles of garden design from Alberti, Michelozzo, Bramante, Vignola, Raphael, Michelangelo?

For more than two centuries the gardens of the

Italian Renaissance lay under a cloud, exciting, it would seem, little but contempt and disgust in all who viewed them. Misson[1] writes in 1688 that in magnificence the gardens of France so far surpass those of Italy, that the best way to save the credit of Frascati and Pratolino is to pass over in silence all the pretty wonders that were once so highly extolled; and speaks with something like contempt of Villa d'Este, which only cost three million francs to build, while the very lead of the canals at Versailles was worth all Tivoli put together. A writer in the *Landscape Annual* for 1831 remarks of Villa d'Este that though delightfully situated, it is deformed by the bad taste in which the grounds about it are disposed. An English traveller, twenty years later, brings a still more sweeping indictment against the gardens of Frascati: they want character and expression, belong to the dark ages of art; with so profuse an expenditure it is wonderful that so little invention has been displayed and that so little beauty has been the result [2].

Let us turn our steps to Italy, and see how far such strictures are justified. These old Italian gardens, with their air of neglect, desolation, and solitude, in spite of the melancholy of the weed-grown alleys, the weary dropping of the fern-fringed fountains, the fluteless Pans and headless nymphs and armless Apollos, have a beauty which is indescribable, producing upon the mind an impression which it is difficult to analyse, to which no words can do justice. In all the world there is no place so full of poetry as that Villa d'Este which formalist and naturalist united to decry. Driving past the little Temple of Vesta, high above the seething cauldron of the Anio, one is admitted through vaulted corridors and deserted chambers where faded frescoes moulder on the wall to a stairway overhanging the garden. And the garden that lies in the abyss below, terrace after terrace looking out upon wooded mountain flank and far mysterious plain—surely Time has forgotten these giant cypresses which lift from the gulf dark pinnacles of night, great rugged, gloomy-verdured spires; surely it is the garden of a dream? Behind one like a cliff rises a palace of romance, vast, august, austere; a palace over which in a far-off age some mighty magician has thrown an enchanting spell of sleep. Sleep and forgetfulness brood over the garden, and everywhere from sombre alley and moss-grown stair there rises a faint sweet fragrance of decay. In the valley below a woman's voice is singing an old-world melody, sad and pure and strange as the Spinning-song of Wagner; a tune which tells of a prisoned soul and the longing to be free. And still one may listen to the magic of the wizard's music, for the muffled thunder of the great cascade dominates the whole garden, and above it, blended like the rolling of the spheres into one deep melodious thrill, are the varying notes of murmuring, mourning, whispering, rioting, rejoicing water.

On the left, the garden looks down upon grey-green olives shot with silver in the sunlight, and upon a vine-clad pergola which clings like a spider's web to undulating slope and dell. Deep drifts of withered leaves have gathered on the stairways, the fountain basins are overgrown with maidenhair or choked with water-weeds, the empty niches draped with velvety moss or tapestried with creepers. Descending by weed-grown stair and crumbling balustrade, one reaches a gloomy alley where a hundred fountains gush into a trough beneath a line of mouldering reliefs. At the further end of the terrace, falling in great cascades like the folds of a Naiad's robe or the flash of a silver sword, the river leaps into the garden, to four great pools of troubled water, a jewelled belt which quivers in the sunlight with a mysterious, an amazing blue. Such is the garden in the sober daylight, but what it may be in the summer nights, when the breath of the ivy comes and goes in waves of drowsy perfume, and great white moths are fluttering about the fountains, and in the ilex arbours and gloomy alcoves there are strange mutterings, and deep-drawn sighs, and whispering voices, and flashes of ghostly white, I do not dare to say.

The Duke of Lante's garden is of another character, a place not of grandeur or tragedy but of enchanting loveliness, a paradise of gleaming water, gay flowers and golden light. The long, straight, dusty road from Viterbo leads at length by a bridge across a deep ravine to a gap in the town walls of Bagnaia, 'twixt Gothic castle and Baroco church, then turning at a right angle in the piazza one sees in front the great Renaissance gateway which opens into the garden. But it is better, if permission may be obtained, to enter the park, and striking upward by green lawns and ilex groves to follow from its source the tiny streamlet upon which pool, cascade, and water-temple are threaded like pearls upon a string. Dropping from a ferny grotto between two pillared *loggias,* this rivulet rises again in an elaborate fountain surrounded by mossy benches set in the alcoves of a low box hedge. Four giant plane trees lift a canopy against the sun, and tall stone columns rising from a balustraded wall warn off the intruding woodland. Thence, running underground, it emerges unexpectedly in the centre of a broad flight of steps between the claws of a gigantic crab—Cardinal Gambara's cognisance—and races down a long scalloped trough, rippling and writhing like a huge snake over the carved shells which bar its passage. From this it drops over the edge of a small basin between two colossal river-gods into a pool below. The fall to the next level gives us a half-recessed *temple d'eau*, with innumerable jets and runlets pouring from basin to basin; and here, flanked by stately plane trees and by the two pavilions which make up the casino, is a grass-plot commanding the loveliest view of the garden. Before us lies a square enclosure jutting out into the vale below, with high green hedges, sweet *broderies* of box bordered by flowers, and in the midst a broad water-garden leading by balustraded crossways to an island fountain which rises like a mount to four great figures of sombre-tinted stone. Water gushes from the points of the star which the naked athletes uplift, from the mouths of the lions by their side, from the masks on the balustrade, from the tiny galleys in which vagrant cupids are afloat upon the pools. It is a colour harmony of cool refreshing green and brighter flowers, of darkest bronze, blue pools and golden light. Much there is of mystery in the garden, of subtle magic, of strange, elusive charm which must be felt but cannot wholly be understood. Much, no doubt, depends upon the setting, upon the ancient ilexes and wild mountain flank, the mighty hedge of green at the further end with its great pillared gateway and the dark walls and orange-lichened roofs of the houses and tower irregularly grouped behind it; upon the quiet background, the opal hues of green, violet, and grey in the softly modelled plain, and shadowy outlines of the distant hills. But the soul of the garden is in the blue pools which, by some strange wizardry of the artist, to stair and terrace and window throw back the undimmed azure of the Italian sky.

The Giusti garden at Verona strikes yet another chord, a motive not of sweet or sombre or tragic, but of intensely solemn loveliness. Driving across the bridge along a dull and dusty street, the carriage stops at a stuccoed house with painted architecture, not much better than the rest. But when the heavy entrance doors are swung back, an enchanted vista holds the traveller spell-bound—the deep, refreshing green of an avenue of cypresses half a millennium old,[1] leading to a precipice crowned by the foliage of a higher garden. For pure sensation there

[1] So one is told; but the garden is first mentioned in 1644 and appears to have been laid out in the sixteenth century, perhaps by San Michele, who added to or altered the house. The older cypresses, one of which was supposed to be seven hundred years old, belonged to an earlier scheme.

is nothing in Italy equal to this first glimpse through
the Giusti gateway. It is but the nature of a single
tree, yet presented with such mastery that the
traveller is inclined to doubt the evidence of his
eyes. "Can it be true," he asks himself, "can anything in the world be so beautiful?" The little
entrance court is bounded by high battlemented
walls, and in the centre tall piers set with obelisks
frame in the view; a gravel walk slopes upward in a
hollow curve between the trees, until the ascent
becoming too abrupt it breaks into three flights of
steps, diminished in breadth in order to increase the
effect of distance: these lead to a dark cavernous
recess in the face of a rocky precipice, planted above
with such a wild riot of jagged cypresses as might
serve for a painted scene of a witches' sabbath.
Toiling upwards through a tower built against the
face of the cliff one reaches terrace walks above, and
a two-storied garden-house, where summer days
may be spent high above the toil and turmoil of the
town. Here, from a projecting balcony, one may
look down upon the venerable trees, upon the green
parterres with their fountains and statues sloping
upwards to the base of the rock, and upon such a
maze of ribbed tiling and crooked streets as may be
seen from many a northern minster tower. Far
away in the blue Lombardic plain lie the domes and

meres of Mantua; the town stretches towards them
in a sea of ruddy-brown roofs breaking round
ancient towers and spires; on the right are the
mountains of the Tyrol, on the left through garden
and vineyard and mulberry-grove runs the faint
blue line of the Adige. Yet it is not to distant city
or purple mountain or bright-flowing river that
memory returns, but to the narrow alley, girt in by
sheer precipices of green, which leads by cave and
turret and winding stair to the secret garden upon
the hill. This little pathway, where twenty generations have come and gone under the shadow of
cypresses tall as the towers of Verona and older than
the oldest palaces, has a grave and haunting beauty
which hardly seems to belong to the existing order
of things: it might have led to the place of an oracle,
to the garden of Plato, the tomb of Dante, the cavern
where sleeps the Venus of the ancient world.

These are the three great gardens of Italy, for the
charm of Caprarola lies only in the Canephoræ—
in the giant guard of sylvan divinities, playing,
quarrelling, laughing the long centuries away,
which rise from the wall of the topmost terrace
against the blue distance of an immeasurable amphitheatre walled in by far-off hills. Isola Bella, again,
is a thing by itself, not a garden, but a mirage in a
lake of dreams; a great galleon with flower-laden

18

terraces and fantastic pinnacles which has anchored here against a background of purple mountains on its return to the realm of rococo. For other work of the first rank we must turn to smaller schemes or to parts of gardens, to the balustraded pool at Frascati, the water-theatre of the Villa Aldobrandini, the lemon grove of the Isolotto at Florence. Of these the last is probably known to every one who has visited Italy. It is an oval lake encompassed by a broad pathway in the shadow of a mighty wall of ilex. Marble seats are set under the green canopy, and quaint baroque fountains from curving shells and gullets of sea-monsters drop tiny rills into the lake, where merman and sea-nymph on water-horses are wildly urging their steeds towards the shore. In the centre of the island a gigantic basin of stone supports three seated figures brackcted against the pedestal of John of Bologna's splendid statue of Oceanus. But the glory of the Isolotto is in its balustrade, where instead of pilasters we have sweeping curves cut away to admit great red garden-vases, which with their burden of green and gold are doubled upon the water film, far above the clouds that are sailing through the blue gulf below.

Villa Torlonia at Frascati is not like Villa d'Este, where the great heart of the Anio throbs through the garden and every grove and thicket and alley is filled with a tumult of sobbing sound. It is a place of mysterious silence, of low-weeping fountains and muffled footfalls; a garden of sleep. The gates are on a lower level, and athwart the rose-tangled slope to the left the architect has thrown five great slanting staircases of stone, broad enough and splendid enough to carry an army of guests to the plateau above. But this is now a solitude, a mournful ilex *bosco* with cross walks and mossy fountains shaped like the baluster of some great sundial. From the central stairway, not far from the house, a broader opening in the woodland leads to a lawn and pool below the great cascade. In front is a long cliff crowned with ilex forest and faced with a frontispiece of moss-grown arches and bubbling fountains. The main fall drops from a balcony between two tall umbrageous ilexes which rise on either hand like the horns of an Addisonian periwig; from basin to basin it drops in a silver fringe, held in by low serpentine walls that curve and re-curve like the arches of a bridge or the edges of a shell. Through vaults on either hand, long winding stairways follow the curves, the masonry is choked with ferns, the steps with weeds, and riotous water-plants crowd upon the ledges or thrust green juicy stems through the scum which has gathered in the corners of the pools. At the top, in a small irregular

20

clearing walled by wild ilex wood and wilder tangle of flowering shrubs, is a balustraded basin in the form of a great *quatrefoil*. Gold-red fish gleam in the sea-green water, which reflects soft foliage and lichened stone and patches of pearly light; in the centre a huge cylinder of moss supports the silvery feathers of a fountain; it is an enchanted pool in a fairy woodland. But the traveller who has wandered here alone on a drowsy afternoon does not linger to listen to the trickle of the fountain and the murmuring of the bees. From below the threshold of the mind a strange sense of hidden danger oppresses him, an instinct neither to be reasoned with nor to be understood. Can there be brigands yet in the forest heights, or is the place haunted by shades of the soldiers who once fell in battle about the pool? He waits and wrestles with his folly, then sadly descending the slippery stairways leaves cooling fount and shaded alley for the torrid sunshine of the outer world.

It is death to sleep in the garden.

For smaller schemes, showing how a great effect may be produced within a narrow compass, the architect will turn to the Cicogna garden at Varese, Villa Gamberaia near Florence; perhaps one should add Villa Bernardini in the neighbourhood of Lucca. Other gardens there are which seem to have worked out the ultimate possibilities of some particular problem. At Bogliaco, on Lake Garda, a road intervenes between the hill-side pleasure-ground and the palace, which is by the shore. On either flank of the house is a little terrace and bridge across the road, walled on the outside to screen the view, and from these bridges walks backed by tall yew hedges sweep round in a semicircle to the central ascent, with its double stairways adorned with arcading and statuary.[1] The public highway, losing its character, has become a private approach. At Cadenabbia, a footpath along the shore cuts off Villa Carlotti from the lake. Here the Casino is on a higher level, balustraded stairways lead down to a circular garden with a graceful baroque fountain, and hedges twenty-five feet high curving forward in plan cover the path, conceal the flat uninteresting water-edge, and concentrate the view. At Castello d'Urio on Como, a late sixteenth-century garden with many statues, a public road offers the same difficulty, which is overcome by a stepped approach and bridge leading to a gate of hammered iron. Villa Borghese at Frascati has a garden at two levels, a great semicircular court disengaging the house and giving light and air to the lower rooms. Castello near Florence and Villa Imperiale at Genoa deal with the difficulties of a

[1] The date of the palace and garden is about 1750

22

sloping site, where the straight walks are on a gentle and easy decline and the terraces lean to the house. Castelazzo, a few miles from Milan, Villas Gori and Sergardi at Siena, Villa Reale near Lucca, Villa Garzoni at Collodi, and the garden of the Castelnuovo Institute at Palermo, illustrate the charm of rustic theatres; Villas Bernardini, Senese, Mansi, Reale, all in the Lucca neighbourhood, the beauty of balustraded pools; the Colonna garden at Rome, Villa Cicogna at Varese, Villa Pliniana on Lake Como, the summer delights of a central cascade; Villas Borghese and Mondragone at Frascati, the advantage, even in the country, of a retired or secret garden on the level of the first floor, opening out of study or saloon.

Of the town gardens first introduced by Epicurus at Athens, Italy furnishes many examples. The Colonna palace at Rome is connected by four graceful bridges with its terraced retreat across the roadway, where fountain and cascade, box, ilex, and cypress cover the giant cornices of the Baths of Constantine. At the Castle of Ferrara, the old terrace-garden is still in existence, and at Mantua there is a *giardino pensile*, supported by five great tunnels of brick; which, however, loses its effect for want of outlook. At Vicenza the garden attached to the Palazzo Bonin slopes upwards at the further end and to the right, where a balustraded terrace over some outhouses leads to a projecting wing occupied by a great saloon. At Genoa there are several gardens raised above the level of the street, as at the Palazzo Durazzo Pallavicini. At Lucca, the fortress-palace of the Guinigi has its garden of flower-beds and ilexes upon the summit of the tower. But the great majority of these palace gardens lie on the level of the street, and there are few of the older cities which will not yield to the passing traveller some glimpse of fairyland, some vista of fern-draped niche or mossy fountain, of Neptune with his trident or Hercules with his club, or of a green *cortile* seen through the rolling curves and rusty scroll-work of a rococo gateway.[1] He is toiling through the hot, dusty street of Verona on a torrid day in June, when fierce sunshine beats back from wall and pavement and roadway; the cool breath of the mountains whispers in his ear, and there through the portal of the Canossa palace lies

---

[1] The traveller must not miss the charming garden-court of the Palazzo Controni-Pini at Lucca, with its statues and fountains and great red earthen jars set against a background of old grey ramparts, nor that of the Palazzo Giustiniani (Via del Santo, 21) at Padua with its loggia and banqueting-house designed by Falconetto; nor those in the Via dei Fiori, Via Moretti, Via Soncino, Via Triest at Brescia. In the town of Como, the Palazzo Giovio, now turned into a museum, has at the end of the garden a terrace commanding a view of the mountain side

the foaming river twenty feet below; beyond it blue vineyard slopes and a chain of snowy peaks: a little terrace, some seventy yards long, overhangs the water, which curves outward to the rose-red towers of the embattled bridge, the brown roofs and fortress walls of the ancient city. Or, on an April morning when the call of Spring is in the air, he is passing along the Via S Marco at Vicenza, in the centre, for all that may be imagined, of a spider's web of tiresome streets, and there through the open doorway of the Quirini palace is the country—swift-flowing brooks and a sweet level of meadowland yellow with buttercups. An avenue of hornbeam on either hand walls out the town, and in the centre a formal approach, a quarter of a mile long,[1] bordered by statues, vases, and green pyramids of *lignum vitæ*, leads to a moated mound crowned by a classic temple. When he has crossed at length the broad, clear water, and is mounting towards the great stone pines which cast their shadow over the building, a fresh surprise awaits him, for, ringing almost three-quarters of the horizon, there rises before his eyes a tremendous amphitheatre of mountains.

Nowhere are these garden vistas more delightful and more varied than at Bergamo, where one

[1] I made it 485 paces to the centre of the mound

cortile looks out upon a long line of giant ramparts curtained with creepers, and bright with red and white valerian and golden snapdragon; another upon a wooded hillside and an enfilade of mountain peaks; another upon a green ocean that stretches as far as the eye can reach, a vast interminable level of mulberry-wooded plain. And there is a peculiar fascination in the upward views through grate and pillared court and further archway deep in shadow, across sunny gardens backed by green foliage of bay or laurel, to the huge grey bastions crowned by chestnut trees, the random tiers of tall red-roofed houses, the towers, belfries and cupolas of the ancient *citta* on the hill. These long vistas which pierce a succession of buildings and enclosures seem to appeal to the sentiment of power, and there is some mysterious charm in the alternation of light and shadow, the contrast of formal masonry and random creepers, in the effect of gloom with light beyond, the seclusion of a secret garden far withdrawn from the dust and traffic of the street. How much do the wayfarer and the poorer town-dweller owe to these delightful confidences, to the mountain breeze which cools the air, the touch of romance which relieves the monotony of city life, and like a rose in winter glows with the promise of a brighter world!

For the dwellers in other cities where nature is

shyer and more retiring, that kindly magician the scene-painter has called lake, mountain and river into the street. Placed behind a pillared screen, with a fountain or strip of garden in the foreground, these landscapes are strangely deceitful. Beyond the *cortile* of the Palazzo Raimondi at Cremona one sees through a tall arch garlanded with twisted stems and smothered with trailing leafage of wistaria and ivy, a distant view of Alpine lake and heights, perhaps of the mountain home from which the family came. Beyond the strip of garden, a boat lies on the beach of the lake, which reflects like a sheet of glass the towers and houses of a little town set in the shadow of a mighty cliff. This scene is painted upon a wall shaped to the profile of the hills. The decorative scheme of the Palazzo Costa[1] at Piacenza, though more elaborate, is hardly so successful. A marble balustrade adorned with statues and urns divides the court from the garden, beyond which is a wall serrated to a mountain outline; but here Time, with his greys and greens and umbers, has followed on the heels of the land-scape-painter, and bridge and terrace, woodland and precipice are mouldering away.

But it is in Brescia, above all places, that the painted vista reigns, for here a southern imagination

[1] Via S Lazaro

has run riot, and the stranger may make his choice of time and place and season, of Goth or Roman, of spring or autumn, of tropic palms or Arctic snows. Here beyond the palace courts are great pointed vaults and ruined castle halls, Renaissance loggias, wild rococo fantasies of pillared porticoes, of crumbling theatres, of interminable arcades. Here are lake scenes with vast planes of stubborn rock lifting themselves into the sky, tiny hamlets clustering round a church tower upon the mountain side, bright palaces gleaming on the water edge, while all the landscape seems to swoon in a white haze of heat. Here on the bosom of a mystic river, leading from nowhere to nowhere, a slow boatman with averted face is ever seeking to raise an unprofitable sail; and here are dreams of the old Roman world before the fall which make one tremble at the sound of a church bell, for by stream or cataract the shepherd is piping to his flock, and under the shadow of the great stone pines shine out the marble statues and temples of the Gods.

Of the principles which guided the great Renaissance garden-makers it is not so easy to speak, for it was in poetry, in imagination that they reigned supreme, and inspiration is a breath of the muses which may not be brought within the rules of art. Their first thought was for the æsthetic impression upon the individual, for sentiment and emotion, for intellectual suggestion, for chords struck upon those vague, nebulous, spectral feelings which are ever trembling upon the threshold of consciousness. To them the garden seemed to be only half the problem, the other half was that blundering ghost-haunted miracle, the human mind. Thus they learnt the value of striking contrast; of sudden and thrilling surprise; of close confinement as a prelude to boundless freedom; of scorching sun as a prelude to welcome shade or cooling river; of monotony, even of ugliness, set for a foil to enchanting beauty, as a discord is used in music, as the lowered tone of a landscape brings out the fires of sunset or the primrose light of dawn, as a dwarfish figure on a Greek sarcophagus gives grandeur to a frieze of fighting heroes. Their work, like that of all great artists, is full of mystery, of haunting beauty, of magic which all must feel but few can understand. Take, for example, the treatment of water. The Italian mastery over the "water-art" has been dealt with by a score of writers, who have failed to notice that a higher poetry may be found in that element than the beauty of form and sound, than the shifting curves of a fountain or the deep-toned music of a great cascade. There is the poetry of colour. Surely some one of these writers must have noticed the

blue of the Vatican fountain,[1] the greenish tint of
the basin at Caprarola, the mysterious reflections of
the water-garden at Lante which strangely and beyond experience mirrors the sky. But, fresh it may
be from the lovely colouring of Como and Maggiore, or from the blue-crystal strand of Garda,
where the sunlight is ever dancing in a magic web
over the pebbles, they have attributed these effects
to any cause but the right one; to happy chance, to
the depth or purity of the water, the clearness of
the atmosphere, the glowing radiance of the southern sun. At the Villa Borghese at Frascati a little
basin some twelve feet across gives away the secret;
the clipped ilex which surrounds it has been planned
to cut off lateral reflections, admitting only bright
sunshine from above; the beauty is due not to accident but to design. These great Italians had learnt
to play with water as a sultan with his jewels, as
Turner played with light; prisoning the blue of the
sea in a tiny pool, the green of the chrysoprase in a
fountain basin, the iris of the rainbow in a crystal
spray; making it glow like a ruby with blood-red
marbles, or quiver in the sunshine with the blue
light of Capri, or throw back as from a mirror the
deeper azure of the Italian sky.

Nowhere, except in Italy, can one learn the

[1] *Dello Scoglio* This has colour even on a sunless day

magnificence of the raised approach. The upward slope at the Marchese Ferrasan's at Savona, bordered by orange-trees in great red vases, must be twenty feet above the garden where it meets the marble terrace, opposite the centre of the house. At Loano, midway between Alassio and Savona, is a still finer approach, an arched bridge great as a Roman aqueduct, connected with what is apparently a small castle. Perhaps the grandest of all is that which leads to the modern Villa Pallavicini at Pegli, where huge retaining-walls of stone a quarter of a mile long and in places not less than sixty feet high lift up a roadway bordered with flowers and shaded by an ilex avenue. For the greater part of its course this road points at a corner of the casino, but presently curves away to the left in order to strike the nearer end of the garden terrace. At the Villa Albertini at Lecco on Lake Como, the sloping stairway of grass and stone has a drop of from six to ten feet on either hand; a difference in level of even a foot is of value, as may be noticed in the Abbondi garden at Riva.

The Italian love of looking down from a height upon a great parterre of flowers finds expression in the Roman gardens of the Vatican, Villa Medici and Villa Pamphili. Another favourite motive in Italian gardens is coolness in the summer heat,

and few of the larger houses are without a grotto
adorned with fountain and marble floor and en-
crusted with sea-shells or fantastic pebble-work.
Evelyn speaks of the rooms under the great fountain in the Pitti Palace, not perhaps so delightful a
retreat as that in the bridge at Blenheim; and describes the water alley at Pratolino, from the sides of
which slender streams rose in the air, making a
perfect vault and falling interchangeably into each
other's channels, so that a horseman might ride
from one end to the other without a single drop
being spilt upon him. The Villa Pliniana near
Como is built in the shade of a wooded cliff upon
a foundation of earth and stones flung down from
above, and through the central loggia a foaming
cascade leaps to the lake, filling the whole house
with the refreshment of its coolness and the tumult
of its sound. At the Villa di Papa Giulio one may
dine in a watery saloon, surrounded by running
streams and bubbling fountains. The court of the
papal Palace at Viterbo hangs in mid-air over a
mighty arch of stone; on either side long benches
are set against an open arcade of interlaced arches,
and to the central fountain water rises from below
through a great octagonal pillar which runs into
the vault. It was built by the wizard Pope, John
XXI, who in 1277 was crushed to death in an

adjoining chamber by diabolic agency, for suddenly as he laughed in pride at the splendour of his work the avenging roof fell in ruin upon his head. To one of the grottoes of the Aldobrandini garden at Frascati secret conduits used to bring in a current of air strong enough to keep a copper ball dancing a yard above the pavement; and here again the whole scheme of house and garden is planned for summer shade and coolness. At the back, a wooded hill almost overhanging the palace has been cut away in a great semicircle to form a rustic theatre of fountains, so that sitting in the great saloon one may see the frigid stream from Monte Algido racing down in cascade and cataract and long sloping aqueduct to two tall pillars of stone, which it mounts in a spiral curve, then falls with the sound of a cannonade upon an heroic figure of Atlas tottering under the weight of a deluged world. Or, turning one's chair, one may look out over the vast stretches of the Campagna, the most impressive plain in Europe, and feel on one's cheek the gentle breeze which plays upon the hillside, blowing from the distant sea.

Even the detail of Italian garden architecture is well worth the study of the designer. For screens or niches to terminate a terrace he will turn to the Imperiali and other gardens at Genoa rather than to Tivoli or Frascati. From many of the villas about

33

Rome, Florence and the Lakes, he will learn to frame in his views and close his vistas with triumphal arches or grand pillared frontispieces which fill the eye; to get on a scale with his stairways, making the risers only of stone, the treads of pebble or gravel or beaten earth;[1] to obtain a rough or rustic surface for niches and great wall-fountains by stones or pebbles embedded in mortar; to make his piers of stately height and his iron gates plain and bold, without ornament except for the curved outline at the top. How inferior are the gateposts at Montacute, at Drayton, even at Hampton Court, to those at Frascati or Albano, or the splendid piers in the Botanic Garden at Palermo! He will learn to relieve plots of turf with statues, and masses of reflected light upon the surface of a pool with mermen on water-horses, or little flower-laden galleys, or cupids astride on plunging dolphins. Villa Arsen at Hyères, the Grand Hotel at Varese, Villa Crivelli at Inverigo will teach him the grace and freedom of wide rococo stairways with curving fronts; Castelazzo, Albissola near Savona and not a few of the Florentine and Roman gardens, the

[1] At Villa Muti, Frascati, there is a good combination of slope and stairway. This is all of stone, and following each step is an incline of double the length. The grass steps at Villa Gamberaia have box borders to cover the ragged edges

[2] See the work at Villa d'Este, Tivoli

warmth and cheerfulness of great lemon-pots[1] in a
box parterre under the windows of the house. Villa
Medici at Rome will show him the importance of
putting sculptured reliefs upon piers and pedestals
and balustrade rests. At Val San Zibio near Batt-
aglia, he will observe the superiority of box hedges
to yew, both for their sweetness and their fresher
green; at Villa Bernardini in the neighbourhood of
Lucca, the grandeur of evergreen walls thirty feet
high which shut out the lowlands and frame in the
mountain vistas.

[1] The largest I have ever seen are at Villa Sormanni, Castelazzo. These
are five feet across and about 4ft 8ins high, made in three portions
and held together by iron rings. Smaller pots containing orange-
trees are lifted into them. In Sicily the mauve flowers of the candytuft
are sometimes used to cover the bare earth in the larger flower-vases

II

THE ITALIAN FEELING FOR SENSATION has often been spoken of. Perhaps the best example of this is furnished by another villa at Frascati, the great sixteenth-century pleasure-house of Mondragone which was built and altered and added to by a succession of popes and cardinals.

From the gate on the Monte Porzio road, a long dark avenue of cypress points at the palace, as a cannon at a star, but the easier and more usual approach is to the right between sweet box hedges shaded by forest trees. Higher up is an ilex avenue, under which the ground is bright in spring with the rose and mauve of the wild anemone and bolder pink of the cyclamen: groves of olive cut off the distant views, and near the house the avenue is doubled and trebled with older, darker, gnarlier

36

trees. The carriage stops between a huge walled recess in the hillside drowned in a cataract of ivy and a plain stuccoed palace-front with simple pillared entrance and square window-frames of stone. Passing through the great quadrangle, remarkable only for scale and austerity, except for a small recessed front at the further end where the Borghese dragons writhe in stone between the pilasters, one enters a gloomy hall and beyond it a small square chamber with painted ceiling and stuccoed figures, a chamber which might be the ante-room to some splendid gallery or imposing saloon, but cannot have been designed as the terminus of so stately an approach. However, there is nothing beyond but a little iron balcony, and after so much gloom and confinement as you step out upon it the boundless view takes your breath away.

Far below the level of the palace windows there opens an immeasurable plain, stretching out mile after mile, league after league, day's journey beyond day's journey, until at last the purple distance melts at the world's edge into a silvery gleam of sea. This immensity of level space is not monotonous, as a meaner plain might be, for it is various in all its parts, embracing rich pasture-lands of feathery grasses and stony desolate stretches, tall pine forests and grave-green marshes, low cliffs and wandering streams; and it is responsive to every mood of the passing seasons or of the flying hours, from the first flush of dawn, when the trailing mist-wreaths rise from marsh, mill-stream and river, until the orange light of midday brightens to gold, and at last the dying day passes away in one vast conflagration of purple and crimson and fiery red. So, too, it changes with the changing year. The golden summer deepens at length to the crimson and purple-brown of autumn and winter; the new year leaps into life in a sudden tide of green; then comes the triumph of spring, when cyclamen and hyacinth, harebell and convolvulus make the war-stained earth like the Garden of Paradise.

The Campagna again is not like the sea, which is dreadful because it remembers not: every bank and hillock has its remnant of tomb or villa or fortress, for this is a wilderness of ruin, a region of shallows which an ebbing tide of human greatness has left strewn with myth and legend; and here under haunted mound or riven tower sleep great cities which have sunk into the underworld, older capitals of Latium, cities which once were rich as Carthage, glorious as Athens, ancient as Tyre. Countless ages have passed since nature swept again over their ruins in a scarlet flame of poppies or a blue tide of April flowers, but the same eternal

stream of life in leaf and blossom is waiting for the
day when Rome too must go down in the abyss of
time; when the red valerian shall flame upon the
altars, green tapestries of matted ivy shall hang
from pillar to pillar; when the climbing rose shall
perfume the churches with its scented showers and
the shrines shall be heaped up with treasure of
golden broom; when the fading saints and martyrs
shall be veiled by bacchanalian vine-wreaths, and
the only music shall be the rustling of the reeds and
the sighing of the grasses, the only worshippers a
heavenly host of flowers.

It is strange what a sense of power and freedom
these mighty outlooks give, lifting the mind high
above all the pettinesses of life, like a night spent
under the stars. For the spirit of man like his body
abhors restraint and confinement, will not be pent
up in a narrow compass nor be content without a
spacious horizon in which the eye may wander and
fancy and memory may move. There is narrow-
ness and madness in these shut-in views of park and
mill-stream and wooded hillside, and a palace to be
fit for thinkers or rulers of men should look down
upon a distant country where one may drink deep
draughts of space and freedom, upon a bay studded
with islands, or at least upon some great river
which, like the stream of Time, bears onwards its

freight of lives and treasure, of human hopes and fears.

This, then, leads up to what I believe to be the great secret of success in garden-making, the profound platitude that we should abandon the struggle to make nature beautiful round the house and should rather move the house to where nature is beautiful. It is only a part of the garden which lies within the boundary walls, and a great scheme planned for dull or commonplace surroundings is a faulty conception, as if one were to propose to build half a house or to paint half a picture. The garden must be considered not as a thing by itself, but as a gallery of foregrounds designed to set off the soft hues of the distance; it is Nature which should call the tune, and the melody is to be found in the prospect of blue hill or shimmering lake, or mystery-haunted plain, in the aerial perspective of great trees beyond the boundary, in the green cliffs of leafy woodland which wall us in on either hand. It may be argued further that real beauty is neither in garden nor landscape, but in the relation of both to the individual, that what we are seeking is not only a scenic setting for pool and fountain and parterre, but a background for life. Natural loveliness at the doors will give a hundred times more enjoyment than loveliness a mile away, and as in the earlier days when every one's parlour was under the sky, when heath and forest and moorland stretched up to the walls of the city and the towers of the castle, health will follow in its train. A garden in a verdurous landscape which strikes a note of beauty and freedom, of exuberant fertility, of happy adaptation to the service of man, will be a nobler gift to the future, more fitted to survive; we shall share in the overflowing happiness of others, and the halo of associations being so much a part of the self that the two can never be disentangled, those who are near to us will shine in our eyes with a reflected light.

There is also to be considered the influence of scenery upon mood and character, an influence so potent that being shown the surroundings of an ancient mansion, one seems to understand at a glance the lives of those who lived under its roof. There are some outlooks that stir the blood like the sound of a trumpet, and others that lull the senses to dreamy and indolent repose. Hamerton's theory is that born in every man is the need of some particular type of landscape, which will throw back to him the light of his own soul in grand or gay or sweet or melancholy beauty; that the lover of liberty will find delight in the vast horizons of the ocean and the desert, while the lover of tranquillity

will sigh for the happy valley of Rasselas or the
island lawns of Avilion; that restless energy will
prefer the brown and rugged grandeur of Salvator
Rosa and indolence or weakness will find repose in
the golden peacefulness of Claude. Undoubtedly
there is a difference between individuals. To some
minds the Campagna is a dismal solitude, a fever-
haunted desert, a nurse of terrible thoughts; to
others it is a miracle of changing beauty, having
just that background of melancholy which makes
happiness more profound. But such a doctrine
seems to allow too much to individual choice, too
little to heredity and early impressions. The High-
lander is as firmly wedded to grey boulder, black
tarn and boding rain-cloud as the Dutch boer to
his trim canals and flat alluvial plain—"who,"
writes Tacitus of the earlier Germany, "would live
in such a wild and rugged country, were it not his
fatherland?" The man is moulded by the landscape
more often than the landscape is chosen by the man.
Indeed, some great poets seem to have become one
with their surroundings, giving expression—one
might almost say consciousness— to the scenery of
a particular district, as an orator gives back in flood
the half-formed thoughts and aspirations which
rise to him in vapour. Thus Wordsworth reflects
the soft vales and shadowy hills and tranquil planes

of light of the English lakes, Perugino the serene sweep of the blue Umbrian uplands. If, then, the landscape has such power over us that it may influence our very thoughts and being, that greatness of soul of which Longinus speaks should be sought not only in the companionship of great men, great books and great pictures, but in looking upon the face of Nature in her grander moods.

The sublime is within the reach of few, the beautiful of many, for in countries such as Italy and Britain the diversity of scenic loveliness and local climate, of soil, rainfall and vegetation, is almost beyond belief. In the north of Scotland there are gardens full of plants which at London would perish from the winter cold. In one Pembrokeshire valley the verbena is a tree of shade, while half a mile away there are shrivelled oaks in a waste of gorse and heather. At Brindisi, the traveller may shiver on the quay in a December wind, while summer is still reigning in the Consul's garden across the harbour mouth. On Lake Maggiore, he may pass at Isola Madre into the Tropics, and look upon strange flowers and shrubs which are hardly to be seen elsewhere in Europe. He may find dismal solitudes, such as that great moor of Rannoch which Hamerton describes, where hundreds of square miles are given over to a chaos-world of blackness and bogs and muddy, melancholy sedges, with one long sinuous lake, dreary as Acheron; and scenes of beauty beyond the power of pen to picture or pencil to portray. Equally amazing are the contrasts of soil, for as there are desolate and blighted valleys where nature seems to lie under a curse; where the tree-forms are gnarled and stunted and nothing flourishes but deadly and ill-omened herbs; where the bushy nightshade is black with its poisonous berries, and gorgeous foxgloves, rank masses of hemlock and nettles, foul henbane, black mullein and stinking horehound run riot as in a witches' garden; so there are happier lands which have come under a double blessing; where the stream of life in plant and tree flows with an added strength, like a brook from the mountain pastures; where the oaks make a mightier bole and giant buttresses uphold the beeches; where the mossy slopes are starred with primroses in spring and in autumn the bracken rises breast-high in a tumbled sea of green and russet-brown and tawny gold. Even for a world-worn man such surroundings will lighten labour and sorrow, will add to the brightness of the sunny hours, and for a child whose senses are yet unblunted, his whole being alive to every impression of beauty, they will heap up a treasury of golden recollections which the Gods cannot take away.

But if we are to seek natural beauty and to follow the senators of the Empire and the cardinals of the Renaissance to the unfurrowed hills, we must not be afraid to build, if occasion demands, high on the mountain side, nor like Lucullus and the storks and cranes to change our habitation with the seasons. How many a modern architect, if such a site as that of Mondragone were proposed to him, would scout the suggestion, pointing out that the place would be bitterly cold in winter, that the cost and labour of carrying up to it luggage, fuel and household supplies would be intolerable; and so the matter would end in a degrading compromise, the client submitting, though sadly, to the superior judgment of his professional adviser, and the house being placed half-way up the slope, where the views are hardly worth having while the inconvenience is almost as great. The Italians of the sixteenth century were wiser than that; they knew the same house couldn't be expected to serve for both seasons of the year; they built for the summer *villeggiatura* and were content to spend Christmas in the town. These great villas at Frascati, Tivoli and Albano were never intended for winter residence. At the present day many men of very moderate means indulge themselves with a summer cottage, and this example is likely to be followed

45

by their richer and less intelligent neighbours, who have more than one residence, but lack the foresight to map out their lives. A house or garden which is expected to look fairly well all the year round can never reach the ideal, and the advantage of knowing during what months it will be occupied and of planning for those months alone is too obvious to be worth discussing.

Next to the choice of site, I would put the maxim that we must subordinate the house to the landscape, not the landscape to the house,[1] making it vast and austere where the note is one of grandeur or ruggedness; sweet and low where nature is in a smiling mood; tall in a level plain; rich with coupled shafts and sculptured friezes and cool colonnades if it faces a quiet prospect; great and dignified in a country of mighty trees. As the house must be related either by harmony or by contrast to the surrounding scenery, so the garden should be in sympathy with them both, the lines being broad and simple against a restless background of rolling

[1] Writers on garden-craft assert that the house is the "one immutable fact" from which everything must start. But those who seek ideal beauty will allow landscape, or landscape and garden in conjunction, to govern the house. It is obvious that where the surrounding scenery offers a quiet background admitting of elaboration in garden design, the house also should be quiet. This does not necessarily mean that it should be plain and unadorned; symmetry and repetition, as at Blickling, will give breadth and repose to a rich façade

hills and dales or where nature has a touch of the sublime, richer, fuller and brighter against a peaceful setting of distant wooded slopes or purple mountains. The climax, as in a picture, may be in the foreground or may be in the background; but cannot be in both.[1] To the house the garden will be as intimately related, for it should be convenient as if one were "stepping from one room to another," and will often carry forward the main divisions or repeat the minor architectural features of the façade; will lay at the feet of the house its brightest gift of flowers and consider in the planning of vista and parterre the outlook from the windows. But the first aim of the designer will always be to consult the genius of the place, to catch the music of

[1] The double climax is particularly unpleasant in a wild and picturesque country such as Scotland, and many old Scotch gardens are ruined by it. Intricacy of design seems to be desirable (1) if the garden, being on a very high site or in a plain, is shut in by foliage or castle walls; (2) if a wooded hillside in the middle distance cuts off the distant views; (3) if the middle distance is eliminated by a falling slope, or by lofty hedges, and the distant country is broad and restful. I am unable to agree with Miss Wharton, whose views however deserve the greatest respect, that the success of the elaborate scheme at Lante is due to the quietness of the distant prospect. I attribute it to the fact that the middle distance is concealed by the hedge and houses immediately behind the garden, and consider that the town of Bagnaia is a background to the garden, and the far distance a background to the town. At Villa Gamberaia, near Florence, the middle views are lost in the falling ground, and far away are the hillsides beyond the broad Arno valley, sprinkled with white-walled villas which give them scale and modelling and human interest

the landscape, and concentrate it by fitting foregrounds and the concealment of defects, whether
it be the blue distance seen between the links of a
low chain of hills, the shadowy gulf of a deep river-
valley, or the green velvet of a mulberry-wooded
plain, a view as at Amalfi along the limestone
headlands of an enchanted coast, or as at Monreale
over a vale where the lemon is ripening in softest
green and palest gold. If it be true that the connection with humanity is the principal interest of
every landscape [3] and will best find expression in
the foreground, then these garden outlooks are the
most beautiful pictures in the world.

Having chosen a site and determined the relation
of house and garden to the landscape and to each
other, we may now consider more closely the in-
ward meaning of our task. The garden, in every
language, speaks of seclusion. To flower and plant
and tree it is a cloistered refuge from the battle of
life, a paradise where free from the pinch of poverty
and the malice of their enemies, they may turn
their thoughts and their strength from war to
beauty; and this perfect freedom of the garden finds
a voice in the joyous murmur of the fountain, for
water too is outside the struggle for existence, and
goes on its way rejoicing from one ocean of dark-
ness to another. So, to man, the garden should be

something without and beyond nature; a page from an old romance, a scene in fairyland, a gateway through which imagination lifted above the sombre realities of life may pass into a world of dreams. One should be able to escape to it from labour or business, from office or Senate-house or study, as to a haven of rest and refreshment, where Time does not dole out his seconds to you like a miser telling his guineas, nor snatch again the golden moments you cannot hold: no sound of the outer world should break the enchantment; no turret-clock should toll the passing hours; nor, could one silence it, should there vibrate through the garden the menacing voice of the church bell, with its muttered curse on nature and on man, lest it beat down the petals of the pagan roses.

All this would be easy enough if we were living in the age of Virgil the Enchanter, or Merlin, or King Roger of Sicily, or Albertus Magnus, or Michael Scott; a few woven circles upon the sand, an earth-shaking spell from the book, and there would be our enchanted fastness, high-walled like the Garden of Mirth in the old romance against pale Sorrow and wrinkled Care and envious Time and all the spectres of the night. But in this un-imaginative age, when a necromancer who ventures even to tell a fortune may be committed as a rogue

and vagabond, it is necessary to be more circum-
spect; we must endeavour to find some form of
"white" magic which does not come within the
meaning of the Act. In a garden, as elsewhere, Art
has the power by selection, accentuation, grouping,
and the removal of defects or superfluities, to
intensify and surpass the beauty of nature, thus
reaching the ideal.[1] This power, being higher than
natural law, is a kind of witchcraft; but it is not the
kind of which I speak. Art has another function
also: it is concerned not only with the scene but
with the mind of the beholder, for more than half
of what we see comes from the mind. Here then
at last we have found the garden-magic of Italy, in
the domain of Psychology—that occult science
which deals in spells, exorcisms and bewitchments,
in familiar spirits, in malign and beneficent influences and formulas of alchemy; that dim untrodden
under-world from which Shakespeare and Wagner
drew their shadowy legions, which will yet inspire
the great poets, artists and musicians of the age to
come. If we use the witchery that here lies ready

[1] The ideal is a concept formed by the perception of differences and
the imaginary prolongation of the direction of such differences to the
furthest point within the horizon of apparent possibility. This point,
or terminus, is the ideal, but it is far short of the horizon of Nature,
which is always transcending it. W James "Principles of Psychology"
i 508

to our hand, the garden, like the work of a great
painter, may "create a mood"; may throw over the
soul the spell of a persisting present, unpursued by a
ravenous past, the child's illusion of an harmonious
universe, free from the discords of sorrow or un-
kindness, from the dominion of iron Necessity or
of scornful Chance; where forethought may colour
the future with rainbow images of spring and hope,
and memory like a fountain pool that has cast off
the dark days of winter can reflect nothing but
flowers and sunshine and deep blue sky. We shall
hear an echo of felicities older than mankind in the
birds' most ancient song, shall know the thrill of
numbers and see in the tender, tranquil eyes of the
flowers, their drooping heads or pouted lips, other
beings like ourselves who may return the sympathy
we feel.[1]

We shall share with all living things that sense of

[1] Personification involves the ascription of feelings. L'Evêque ("La
Science du Beau," 1872, pp 93-4) makes a wave of affection for the
object part of the emotion of beauty, and I think that in one's own
garden there is an illusion of a return wave. The pleasure we derive
from colour, scent, and song in the garden is a bye-product of
evolution, due to that similarity of environment and of the power to
respond to it which has cast our senses almost in the same mould with
those of the insects and birds; and the significance of the fact is that
life is one and man a part of nature, not a supernatural being who has
been suddenly intruded into a garden. The discovery that some plants
have rudimentary sense-organs, and that the cell nucleus is capable of
memory and desire, must revolutionise the whole science of
psychology

union with Nature which is the very essence of pleasure—in the radiant happiness of the plants whose flowering is the expression of a desire to live, a sigh of well-being, a smile of thankfulness, a hymn of praise, whose blossom is as laughter and whose perfume is as song, and the sight of all these smiling faces will teach us that life is a splendid gift, not a vale of tears but a dell of roses. We shall learn the philosophy of the plants, which have ceased from their wanderings, which do not seek to shiver in the cold shadow of impending ill, to groan in anticipation under evils which are beyond remedy and evils which may never arise, to guard against the future by building up an organ of instability, an organ of suffering, but have made their peace with Destiny, resigning themselves in hope and trustfulness to their winter sleep. We shall learn the inmost secrets of the garden, the hidden relations, the waves of mysterious affinity that flow between these flowers that cannot thrive except in the company of their kind, the green thoughts of the trees whose leaves are trembling at the sough of the distant rain, Spring's first "faint beatings in the calyx of the rose." So, as time goes on, the glamour of the garden shall deepen, till we know that it is a commonwealth and that we are citizens with the rest. The great trees cast their

shade over the garden, which shields them from
the woodman's axe; man gives in labour what he
takes in beauty, and every bush and flower has its
appointed task, for there are some that feed the min-
strels or find their dole of honey for the marriage-
making bees, that watch through the midnight
hours or guard the thickets with thorns and prickly
blades and snares of coiling cables; and some there
are that worship the Sun God, following in silent
adoration his progress through the sky, and some
that breathe a perfumed prayer at morn or even,
when he scatters from his chariot the soft roses of
dawn, or returns like a conqueror to his flaming
city in the west. Thus it seems that one interest
binds the garden together, one desire runs through
it, a common purpose animates the whole: to dream
through the dreary winter, when the petals of the
cloud roses are drifting down in sheets of chilly
blossom, when the boughs of the leafless woodland
are heavy with crystal fruit, then, when the dream
is over, to wake again, to creep out from the dark-
ness, to bask in the sunshine of another year.

But if we are to call up this new world of mists
and shadows to replace the illusions of the old, it
will be necessary to face the problems of psychology, and in the first place to analyse the pleasure
which the beauty of a garden gives. There is no

truth but the whole truth concerning an object, both in its countless aspects and manifold relations, and what we call the garden is only a single, fugitive appearance, an infinitesimal part of the whole; not a reality, but a phantom which we mistake for a reality. It is not even a part of the truth, all we know with certainty of such existences in the outer world being that in every quality and feature they are utterly unlike our conception of them. A rose is neither red nor sweet though we may think it so. To the old man, time and space and colour are not the same as they are to the boy. For the tiny creatures that swarm in a dewdrop and may swim in thousands through the eye of a needle, the garden has no existence; it is beyond the grasp of their minds, beyond the ken of their senses, further off than the clustering suns of the Milky Way. For the blind man it is a dull place; not a sight, but a sequence of touches with feet and hands, a succession of perfumes, of lightly echoed sounds, of the perception of obstacles and open spaces; a place of soft turf, warm sunshine and whispering breezes. The thing itself with him is the chain of touches, the other impressions are only signs of the thing: if you could show him the garden he would not recognise it. For the smaller winged inhabitants of the flower-land, which make ten or fifteen thousand wing strokes in a single second and are supposed to be conscious of every one, time moves by another measure, the day is a twelve-month long and gravity a restraint as light as it may be to the dwellers upon Mars. To their eyes, which reach beyond the violet rays, the world is full of colour which we may not see, to their ears of rhythms which we may not hear, calls and love-songs and shrill alarms and rustling music of unfolding leaves and pistol-shots of bursting bud or falling berry; and other senses they may have [4] which the heart cannot even conceive, differing from ours as light from heat or sound from motion. They indeed must find it such a wonderland as we have dreamed, an enchanted forest of fearful delights, where trees a thousand feet high are laden with flowers of incredible magnificence, roses great as arbours, snowy cupolas and purple obelisks, spires of red-crocketed blossom, peals of azure bells; with cup-like flowers that offer fairy foods—ambrosia, and draughts of nectar and chalices of poison; where skiffs with painted sails come floating down the breeze, and nets of corded silk are gemmed with globes of rainbow crystal, and in the green light of the thickets lurk forms of unearthly beauty or of uttermost horror—dragons in jewelled mail or burnished armour, horned dinosaurs, and filthy creeping monsters; where the flying moments flow with a soft gliding, like weary watches of the night, and giant magicians pass onward with imperceptible motion, slow as the snowy clouds that steal through the summer sky.[1]

To human beings, from whom all these marvels are hid, the beauty of a garden is less enthralling, the pleasure less acute. It is what is termed a massive and soothing pleasure, built up of many strands of feeling. There is the pride of the eye in colour and curving lines and dappled light and shade; the suggestion of pleasing rest and coolness; the intel-

[1] The object-world of the insects differs strangely from ours. It is a miracle-world in which nothing happens by law, in which the extraordinary freshness of sensation makes sensuous beauty greater, though symbolic beauty be less. Scent is the dominant sense of the insects, enabling them to distinguish not only a greater number of odours, but the direction, motion, and even the shape of the objects from which such odours spring. Their sight is supposed to be quicker than ours for movement, but less distinct for form. The ultra-violet rays, which with human beings are absorbed by the lens, constitute, as Lubbock points out, for some insects a new and unimaginable colour, differing from violet as green from blue or red from orange, and if these rays enter into the composition of white light and the red are absent, the general aspect of nature cannot be the same. The relative value of colours may also be changed. With our eyes the sensitiveness to green is three hundred and seventy times as great as that for red: with the insects, for all we know, some other colour may be raised to the higher power. Further, it is possible that some insects possessing organs the use of which is unknown may have a sixth sense. Between forty thousand vibrations of the air in a second, giving the highest audible sound, and four hundred million vibrations of the ether, giving the sensation of red, there is room for many unimaginable senses

lectual pleasure of the processes of comparison and deduction; the train of association which calls up memories of other gardens, of other trees and flowers; the appeal to the sympathetic sentiments of power and happiness,[1] whereby we rejoice in another's good fortune, finding delight in the vigour and well-being of plant and herb and tree. Further, there is the gratification of the instinctive sympathy of reason, where the scene has the qualities of appropriateness, diversity in unity, proportion, symmetry or balance, orderly progression, all of which come under the head of design, or at least of order and fitness. In every well-planned garden, as indeed in every work of art, there are many harmonies of appropriateness—in relation, convenience, proportion or scale, form, colour, historic style—so subtle as to escape individual notice;[2] but these come within the halo of obscurely felt relations, and being fused together rise above the threshold of consciousness in a vague and general

[1] See the writer's unpublished essay on beauty, in which it is shown that in addition to the recognised elements of æsthetic pleasure, there are in the mind natural sympathies of power, freedom, happiness, and reason, and emotions or passions of ideality and personality '

[2] It is to these harmonies that Michael Angelo must have been referring when he spoke of spoiling his music. Many things which do not come within the field of our ordinary consciousness are recorded in the lower conscious centres. See Forel, "The Senses of Insects," p 298

sense of ordered beauty. Art's highest appeal to emotion is in the region of sub-consciousness.

Up to this point we have dealt only with the impressions which reach us through the avenue of sight, but the influence of the other senses in a garden is not so trifling as might at first appear. It has often been observed how the impressiveness of natural scenery is heightened by some sound in harmony with the landscape, by the scream of the eagle in the mountains, the howling of wolves in the forest, by the goatherd's piping, the carols of harvest home, the song of the nightingale, the trembling music of the vesper bell. Alison considers such sounds to be sublime[1] or beautiful only from association, the mind connecting them with certain qualities and certain scenes: but the power they have over us would rather seem to be due to the suggestion of life and force and movement, to the tightened grip of reality, the shock of surprise, to something which Nature here uses with a success beyond the reach of orator or rhetorician —the device of impersonification. The landscape,

[1] The sublime is an emotion raised by overwhelming power or magnitude or duration of time; that is to say, overwhelming in comparison with our own insignificance. There is thus sublimity of power, freedom, height, length, vastness, and duration, which may or may not be mixed with beauty. In the presence of the sublime, the consciousness of self is lost (Spencer, i 231,ii 438; pars 98,439), and all irrelevant and trivial ideas are excluded

as you gaze upon it, has found a sudden voice. It is speaking—telling you the wild delight of savage freedom, the fervour of the chase, the careless Eden of the upland pastures, the thankfulness of harvest, the rapture of requited love, the tranquil sadness of the dying day. So lofty a string of emotion may not be stirred in a garden, where sublimity, if it be reached at all, can only be the sublime of nature beyond the boundaries; but the peaceful murmur of a fountain placed at the climax of the scene may heighten its prevailing note, the rush of water will give life, and statue or fountain masks may add the crowning interest of personality. Other sounds and the stirrings of other senses—the warbling of birds, the sighing of the wind in the tree-tops, the myriad-tongued murmur of the lime-blossoms, the perfumes of free-scented flowers, the soft and springy turf, warm sun and breaths of vagrant air —each of these has its share in building up the impression we receive.[1] The eyes, owing to the

[1] The softness of turf gives a light heart, and sounds which repeat themselves, such as the bubbling of a fountain, the cawing of rooks, the song of the cuckoo, strike a note of peacefulness. The total impression of a garden is built up not only of sensation interpreted by perception, but also of sentiment and emotion, and the interest of the house, the beauty of the landscape as seen from the garden, the character and historical associations of the surrounding country, even the circumstances under which one first visited the place, have a share in shaping it. Such an impression is an indivisible whole and the sentiment attached to it makes it distinctive as a chord in music

variety of their functions and the power of dealing with many objects at once, must always be the dominant sense, but being on duty for fully sixteen hours out of the twenty-four, they are apt to fall into a kind of waking slumber. The ear, on the other hand, has so much leisure that it is alive to every sound, and having originally been employed to give warning of danger, as is shown by the infant's fear of noise, it instantly awakes the mind. Thus aroused, the brain uses the eyes to greater advantage, selecting among a countless multitude of new impressions those which bear upon the subject of thought. The sense of smell has also its peculiar province, a strange power of conjuring up the past,[1] being bound up with memory because at some early stage of racial development it has been, like the sense of taste, necessary for the protection of life; and we shall therefore carry away a lasting

[1] In addition to the pleasure of sensation, there is a vague and baffling suggestion of other delights. This is probably due to re-representation below the threshold of the joys which other gardens have given. As with wild animals a certain scent will render nascent in idea the motor changes which accompany the running down, seizing, killing and eating of the prey, so in this case the memory of other experiences is stirred, but so faintly that it eludes our grasp, like a name we cannot quite recall. Sometimes the actual scene may be reproduced. Compare Spencer's "Psychology," 1870, i 61, 191, 308, 484; ii 638 (pars 22, 76, 140, 214, 536). There seems also to be a suggestion of flavour, the very message the flowers are sending to the bees; and indeed smell must be considered as taste at a distance, just as sight is distant touch. Grant Allen points to the dwindled olfactory lobes as proof that smell is an

recollection of the garden, if round the fountain of which we have spoken the air is heavy with the scent of some particular flower, or succession of flowers, if "the woodbine spices are wafted abroad and the musk of the rose is blown." But the chief work of the other senses in a garden is to heighten the feeling of reality, without which we cannot really understand nor know nor enter into possession, for as in reading and even in thinking we are assisted to grasp the meaning of the symbols by mental images of the feeling of articulation and of the sound of the words, so these sensory impressions of sound, scent and touch tighten our grasp of the object and adding the criterion of reality, the power to inflict pleasure or pain, make it part of the one ultimate fact, the consciousness of our own existence. With the eyes a double impression at slightly varying angles gives a striking perception of solid

atrophied sense which has outlived its principal uses, and considers that it now yields relatively large emotional waves and relatively small intellectual information; in fact, that it has sunk into a sentimental old age. Many flowers which are wind fertilized exhale perfume, and according to Maeterlinck the original function of perfumes is unknown. I venture to suggest that it was to lessen evaporation, scented air being opaque to the heat rays. If perfumes are to be described by poets or scientists, new terms must be invented; in the rose alone seventeen different varieties of scent have been distinguished by experts, and to find a proper epithet for the odour of the box leaf we should have to combine the adjectives warm, sweet, bitter, clean, aromatic effect, and how much stronger is the conviction of truth when we have approached the scene from so many, from such widely different sides; when the senses in conjunction, like a party of experts in a laboratory, have tested it for light, colour, form, motion, space-distribution, distance, and magnitude; for the freshness of the air, the chemical constituents of flower and grass and tree; for the signs of sunshine, wind and turf; for the intensity, the volume, continuance, tone, clearness, harmony, rhythm, character of the sounds, and the evidence they give of distance, direction and movement.

Thus the other organs of sense combine to strengthen belief and possession, to heighten the enjoyment of the eyes; pleasure gives an added force to energy and vitality, and the whole man is more alive; beauty rouses emotion, emotion unlocks the door to imagination, which is set free to wander in a world of dreams. Thus in the flowing tide of happiness, which has as much power to intensify reality and impressionability as melancholy has to diminish them [5], the constraints of trouble or pre-occupation or self-consciousness are swept away, and following the general law that one great pleasure fires all the pleasurable sensibilities, the delights of the intellect, of society, music, poetry, even of food, exercise, and rest, are nowhere so vivid as in a garden. The golden lesson of Psychology is among the many selves to choose the best, and in such surroundings a new character is put upon the individual, sympathy is exalted, all the powers of the mind are at their brightest, and the acuteness of feeling is in itself a joy. Ruskin [6] and Alison make too much of raising a train of imaginative thought, which may heighten but cannot cause the enjoyment of beauty that we feel at the first glance; and indeed the delight which landscape gives is due chiefly to the elevation of mood, lifting the mind out of those gloomy realms where sorrow and suffering or disappointment or anxious foreboding have gathered round them the spectres of past unhappiness, above this object universe of double-faced pleasure and pain, to a world of sunshine where Beauty reigns over the shadows of the happy hours, and every shadow is a friend.

III

IT WILL BE ASKED PERHAPS WHAT scientific basis there is for all these pretty theories, and in order to prove that the danger is not that one should be too imaginative but that one should not be imaginative enough, I must turn for a moment to the physical process of which consciousness is the other side. The higher centres of sensation in the cerebral hemispheres are storehouses of old impressions [7], and those which have often been in action together become connected[8]: we have therefore, answering to each cluster of qualities and relations frequently met with in the outer world, an organised group or *plexus* of cells and fibres in the brain, of which if any part is stirred the wave of nervous excitement will tend to spread to the rest. Let a fresh cluster of a kind

64

already known unexpectedly offer itself—say the view of a garden—and the recognition of it as belonging to a particular class will involve the faint revival in memory or idea of [i] the aggregate of past impressions, and [ii] the knowledge grouped about them; in this case all that gardens have meant to countless generations of human beings, the flower language of love, flowers as the universal symbol of beauty and motive of ornament, the pathos of the faded rose, the Idyll of Ausonius and Ben Jonson's rendering of it, the garden lore of Herrick, Vaughan, and Herbert, the flower imagery of Milton and Shakespeare, of Keats and Shelley. These ideas, or others like them, will be in the background of consciousness [9], not in the focus of intellectual sight but in the "fringe" or "halo" of obscurely felt relations; belonging rather to feeling than to knowledge [10]; below the horizon themselves, but rolling up above it a mist of sentiment out of which at any moment trains of conscious thought may spring.

This is not all. The centres which deal with sensation and emotion being the same, a faint stirring of past experiences involves also a more vivid renewal of [iii] the emotion common to such past experiences and [iv] of other feelings of pleasure which have been accidentally associated with

them.[1] In our garden melody of delight we have
thus in addition to the gratification which is found
in the exercise of eye and ear and brain, in the prospect of investigation and comparison, in the calling
up past impressions crowned with a garland of sentiment and knowledge, and the troupe of pleasurable
emotions which dance attendance upon them,—the
echo of a counterpart; a re-representation of the
fresh gladness of spring, the joy and wonder of
a child's heart, the ease and freedom of other
hours spent in the garden, the happiness experienced
in the companionship of parents, playmates and
friends, sympathy felt in the pleasure of others;
and beyond these chords, mysterious overtones,
fainter echoes from the immeasurable past, dim
ancestral reminiscences of emotions stirred by the
freer life of mountain and river, of the forest and
of the chase [11]. Even this is not all, though already the process goes beyond comprehension and
almost beyond belief. The reproduction in idea
of past feelings tends to revive, not only others

[1] Spencer's "Psychology," i 492; ii 594, 641 (pars 216, 519, 537).
In this revival of other associated feelings of pleasure, it must be
presumed that the senses of hearing and smell play an important part,
these having greater power to gather round them accretions of mood
and sentiment, though impressions of sight are more easily reproduced
in memory. Every one has noticed the feeling roused by the cawing
of rooks, the perfume of new-mown hay, the voice of an old friend
heard unexpectedly

accidentally connected with them, but [v] all others of the same class [12]. So, the masses of plexuses in the brain which deal with impressions inter-mixed with pleasurable emotion being intimately connected and the nervous discharge following the lines of least resistance, other feelings of beauty and happiness are partially aroused, there is a dim representation, vague, massive, multitudinous, of all kinds of pleasure, and an indefinable sense of well-being [13].

To these delights of a garden age may add a further interest which can hardly be distinguished from beauty, for the mind, at least with those who have the historic instinct, is always longing to be connected with the past, and dreading for itself con-finement upon the plane of time, delights in evid-ences of the long continuance of nations, families and institutions, in hale and vigorous old age, in long-settled peace beyond the turn of Fortune's wheel, the "scornful dominion of Accident." Rest-fulness is the prevailing note of an old garden; in this fairy world of echo and suggestion where the Present never comes but to commune with the Past, we feel the glamour of a Golden Age, of a state of society just and secure which has grown and blossomed as the rose. How few there are who are incapable of feeling the mysterious appeal of such a place—of the scenes which reflect upon us the passion and the happiness of bygone generations, the statues which gleam out under the deepening spell of the twilight like phantoms of old-world greatness, the still pools that slumber in the sunshine and call our spirits to their dreamland of abiding peace, the rippling music of the fountain, like trills of elfin laughter, and the hoarse water-voices that are hasting with passionate earnestness to the everlasting sea. But beyond all this there is a deeper mystery. In such scenes there is the same elusive suggestiveness that is found in the perfume of the flowers. That which is interesting is real [14], and the old garden is very real. It has the power of fixing attention, it grips you by the sleeve, it is instinct with a silent eloquence; you feel in the Spiritualist phrase that it is "seeking to communicate," to open vistas into the past, that it has a secret to unfold, a message to deliver. What then is this secret of the old-world garden? This,—that it knows us well. We have come back to an earlier home, to scenes which are strangely familiar to us, to the life of former generations whose being was one with ours. Every living creature is adapted to its environment by changes in brain structure produced either by the natural selection of accidental variations or by multitudinous repetition of the same impressions and the same actions. It is this harmony with the surroundings which we feel upon entering an old house or garden; vague ancestral memories are faintly stirred[1] and the sentiment which may attach to objects that have been habitual sources of enjoyment to generation after generation [15]. If by long hereditary connection pleasure has thus become associated with a child's doll [16], it may be with a flower or even with a garden; and more particularly with a garden that represents the ideal world of our forefathers, reflecting the care and forethought, the high unselfish endeavour, the ordered symmetry, the simple quaint formality of their lives. Architecture, far more than poetry or any of the sister arts, is a "strong conqueror of the forgetfulness of men." History and romance may leave us cold and unconvinced—the past of which we read or hear is far away; but let the primordial sense of touch extended by sight be brought into action, with its stronger grip of reality,[2] its greater precision, its fuller information—let our hands handle and our

[1] I think that instinct in animals will some day be explained as inherited memory in the form of idea; that is to say, an inherited tendency for a certain tract in the brain to react to a particular stimulus. Spencer draws practically no distinction between memory, idea, and desire ("Psychology," par 213)

[2] Those things are real which are judged by our senses to belong, like the body, to the world of space; that is to say, not to the world of things as they are, but to the world of things as they feel

eyes behold the homes of our ancestors, and instantly we are back in the life of earlier days. We are dealing no longer with mental images—homeless wanderers in the world of space disowned and rejected by all around—but with the thing itself; thoughts which are almost memories flash upon the mind, a host of associated facts take their places in the scene, and before us there rises the majestic pageant of the past.

It has been observed of the sham rivers introduced into English parks by Capability Brown, that when once the two ends have been discovered, they have lost for ever their beauty and their power to please. As continuance is part of the idea of a river, so it is of a garden, and no new pleasure-ground will satisfy the mind unless we may see it both as it is and as it is to be, when the hedges have shot up into fortress walls of green, and flowering weeds have rooted themselves in the crannies, and the lichen is creeping over the balustrades in a slow tide of curdled foam; when the robes of Nymph and Naiad are damasked with gold and silver blooms, and old associations are gathering in the garden, thickly as autumn leaves. A garden, like a building, must be stable in appearance as well as in reality, must have the restfulness of assured position; the glory of youth is in its promise as of age in its memories. If the scheme has no air of permanence, no wall of defence against the gipsy horde of briars and brambles which is waiting to break into the forbidden land, to pitch its tents on the paths, and riot over the lawns, and pluck down the flower-vases; if it mourns an unsettled or a gluttonous age, which takes no heed of the morrow; if it despairs of the future, preaching the uncertainty of life and the uselessness of effort—the cup of beauty it offers will be tainted with sadness. In our flower-fastness there must be solid evidence of lime and stone that the labour of the builder has been for others; for after-generations who shall mix its music with their joys and sorrows, with their hopes of the future and their memories of the past.

Whenever we look at a picture, we are entering a new world of imagination, leaving the real and turning to the ideal. So it should be with a garden, and to proclaim it boldly as a kingdom of romance we may people it with figures of Olympian deities, with virtues and graces, wood-nymphs and dell-nymphs, dryads and satyrs. Even the topiary works of the Renaissance, the green ships and helmets, giants, dragons and centaurs, had something of reason to recommend them, for by their very strangeness they would be likely to compel atten-tion, to stir imagination, to strengthen memory, to banish the consciousness of self and all trivial or obsessing thoughts. The frontiers of this fairy kingdom must be clearly marked by ramparts strong enough to prevent intrusion, but not in such a way as to shut out the distant landscape. One of the great lessons of psychology is the importance of trifles, and when all our labour is done we may find the eye returning again and again, not to fountain or lawn or parterre, but to some object so trivial that it can be hidden by a single finger of the outstretched hand; some tiny cloud of blue which tells of a far-off mountain, some gleam of distant water half seen between the trees, or green depth of a forest glade. The fascination of such sights, whether due to the excitement of wonder, the ancestral call of wild nature [17], or the charm of mystery in a landscape where something should always be left to fancy and to desire [18], is too strong to be resisted; the whole lay-out should be subordinated to them, and on no account should they be cut off by a rigid boundary, the "good high wall for choice" of the English architects.

The garden, like every other work of art, should have a climax, which may be emphasized by moving water or by reflection, by higher light and deeper shadow, by colour, elaboration in design, or by sculpture which adds the charm of personality;

and whatever this focus of interest may be, whether
it stirs the emotion of sublimity by the prospect of
mountain amphitheatre or plunging cataract or
measureless infinity of plain, the emotion of beauty
by immemorial cypresses, by lake or river valley,
blue pool or fountain basin, it must be presented
with what is known as "economy of the recipient's
attention" [19]; that is to say, without the addition
of features which disturb or detract. If a picture be
complete, everything that is added is something
taken away. The Law of Novelty will teach us not
to fritter away the effect in half glimpses, but to
deliver it with unsullied freshness, like a knock-
down blow straight between the eyes; for it is a
fundamental principle that no second occurrence
of any great stimulus can ever be fully equal to the
first. The power of novelty to "quicken observation,
sharpen sensation and exalt sentiment" [20] is as
marked as that of familiarity to throw a veil over
ugliness [21]. Surprise may add to novelty the
shock of contradiction, and if care has been taken
to make the expectation less than the reality, we
shall have the added thrill of wonder. Indeed, in
every great garden there should be some element
of wonder or surprise, if only to make recollection
more vivid [22]. We shall learn, again, from the
Law of Relativity that as the emotions of beauty,

73

sublimity, novelty and freedom represent in each
case a change in consciousness from the less to the
more pleasing, so either of them may be heightened
by contrast, that is to say, according to circumstances, by an ugly, commonplace, monotonous,
or confined approach. In the opposition of sunshine to the coolness of shade and water, another
principle is involved, for the actual bodily discom-
fort heightens reality, and the mind attaching little
value to that which has cost it nothing, we shall do
well, though Bacon is against us, to buy our shade
by passing through a few yards of sun. Contrast
again may take another form which brings it under
the head of harmony; that is to say, the opposition
to each other of pleasing qualities which it thereby
makes more distinct and noticeable, as of lofty
terrace to low parterre, of studied order to wayward negligence, of massive strength to tender
grace.

Such a harmony of contrast is especially valuable
at the garden boundary. For this reason the mossy
pillars of the woodland, where it beats against the
garden, are to be wreathed with a wild tangle of
ivy and vine, of hop or honeysuckle or convolvulus,
and the trees themselves to be such as affect a rough
and rugged form, gnarled oaks with a hydrabrood
of writhing arms or rugged elms or knotty chest-

nuts; for this reason we are to avoid a multiplication of enclosures, which destroys the background of the picture, throwing back too far from the house the contrast between the wild riot of rebellious nature and the Roman peace of art. Bacon's gardens of the months may be suited to the promenades of a city park, but are not to a private nor even to a royal garden. If spaciousness is desired, it will best be obtained by carrying forward the axial line, or main alley, along a canal or cascade or *tapis vert* of green turf, a plan equally appropriate for the manor-house and for the palace.

Straight lines, according to Ruskin, are valuable because they suggest restraint and set off by their monotony the freedom and variety of natural curves: it follows that flowers will be fairer in formal beds, wild foliage when opposed to massive masonry. Indeed, irregularity and diversity naturally confuse and bewilder us, having no beauty of their own, but only by contrast with a background of order and unity. Symmetry, which gives a sense of rest, will be the law of the garden, the human mind being prejudiced in favour of simplicity and rhythmic recurrence [23], but symmetry too exact is a characteristic of dead rather than of living things, as in the latter it is never quite perfect and is disguised by movement. With gardens, as with buildings, life and freedom are given to the plan by slight aberrations from the square which can hardly be perceived unless they are sought for [24]. It is surprising how much real freedom is wrapped up in the old formality. The circular endings of the terraces at Hampton Court and Helmsley conceal the awkward return of the paths which run into them. The star-shaped parterre in the Colonna garden at Rome covers a corner entrance. The plans of Caserta, Palazzo Borghese, Isola Bella, the Vatican and Boboli gardens, Levens and Melbourne in England, show how easy it is to disguise a change of direction. At Villa d'Este the designer has twisted the great descent of his central alley some yards to the left, caring little that the squalid houses of the town should encroach upon the corner of his garden and even cross its middle line. At Fenarola, a late eighteenth-century garden near Brescia, a bolder divergence from rectitude is concealed by what one can only describe as a heartless fraud. Behind the house is a formal ascent on the hillside, interrupted in the centre by an octagon, the lower flights of steps being steeper than those above, so that it is impossible to see both series at once. Within this octagon, masked by the sweep of a double stairway, the axial line changes very considerably, to suit the plane of the higher hillside; but the visitor only discovers the trick on the high-road, half a mile from the house, and drives away with an uncomfortable feeling that the architect has been laughing at him.

Of statues in the garden, Bacon has written that they are for state and magnificence, but nothing to the true pleasure of it; and Temple could see little in them, or rather in the stone of which they are made, beyond a suggestion of coolness in the summer heat; yet from this faint and damning praise we may appeal to Wagner's great rule that as far as possible all the arts should be used in conjunction, and to Spencer's judgment that the highest æsthetic feeling is roused by the exercise of many powers [25]. Let sculpture add yet another appeal to emotion, and the pleasure stirred by beauty in a garden may rise from massive to acute. It is not only that the statues will set off the garden; we have to consider also that the garden will set off the statues, crowning them with a garland of beauty they could not have elsewhere. Further, there is the opinion already so much insisted upon, that the designer should aim at the ideal, not merely at that low form of ideality which goes beyond nature in the perfection of shape and colour and arrangement, of leaf and blossom, turf and tree, but at the nobler kind that mixes imagination with beauty, taking us into a new world of romance out of all relation to experience and knowledge. In a modern picture-gallery, nothing is so refreshing as to turn from the dreary realism of modern landscapes to scenes whose character is boldly asserted by imaginary figures of satyrs or water-nymphs or centaurs. The original function of imagination seems to have been to prepare us in childish play for the battle of life and in manhood to enable us to foresee and guard against future dangers, and like other useful faculties this requires exercise and pays for it in pleasure. There is thus a natural emotion or passion of ideality, which craves to be satisfied, and every man in his own way must seek the ideal, whether he find it in church or library, in art or music or literature, in the cell of the monastery or the cave of the recluse, or in that flowery land where beauty has forgathered from the very ends of the earth.

This grown-up playfulness of the imagination finds encouragement in the fact that mankind, who spend a third of their lives in dreamland, give also much of their waking hours to imaginary worlds— to the world of appearances, the world of wrong ideas and popular errors and superstitions in which they cannot fail to believe, the various worlds of religion, more real in sickness than in health, the worlds of romance, which they only pretend to believe in. Imagination loves to be employed, and is so absorbed in the interest of ideal relations that it will shut its eyes to minor discrepancies, if only we can avoid the affront of an unnecessary contradiction; pleasure again helps to occupy the mind with the object, excluding all hostile influences. We do not see the unnatural lighting in the picture, the supporting blocks in the sculpture, the audience that sits about us: we are not even surprised when great Cæsar on the stage declaims in modern English. These enchanted scenes of theatre, opera and academy do not actually command belief, but are real to us while we look upon them with the reality of similitude which has not reached its highest point, exact equality; for reality is only an assertion by the senses and the perception that the object belongs to the outer world of existence and is what it appears to be, while belief is a settled judgment that such an assertion is true. Consciousness of the outer world is a very complex thing, depending upon the excitation, not of a single centre, but of a great group or plexus of nerve cells and fibres which varies with every object, and some of these centres may be actually deluded, while in others the sensibility is only partial or latent. The mind cannot deal with more than one idea at a time, though three or four others may lurk in the background

79

of consciousness. Somewhere in the very plexus occupied in putting before us an impression of the scene, is a brain tract which, if fully irradiated, will present us with the profound reflection that all these things are only painted shows; but its protests have been scouted, its warnings have been disregarded, it has been lulled to sleep.

But to return to the question of sculpture. Statuary proclaiming the imaginative ideal may strike in the garden a keynote of wonder and romance. The only rules it is necessary to observe are that there should be a background of mystery and obscurity, such as a forest or a great plain or a chain of distant mountains may give; a well-defined boundary; a shock of delight or surprise to lift us over the threshold of fact; an air of grandeur or distinction in the garden itself and in all its parts [26]; that we should not mix the worlds of romance, but should admit only one supernatural, other circumstances being congruous with it and with each other; that we should leave as much as possible to the mind, because imagination flies from a finished picture and loves to accept a bare sugges-tion [27], filling in the details for itself. But even where conditions do not favour the ideal, a pleasure-ground, however small, should have its presiding genius, its Nymph of flower-garden or

grove or woodland, or Naiad of the Well, appealing to that other emotion of personality [28] which induces the mind to be ever looking for some being like itself, some face among the rocks or figure in the branching wood, to give a personal interpretation to the forces of nature and to feel in lake or mountain or forest the thrill of a living presence. This emotion, springing perhaps from the primal dread of solitude, forms a fresh bond between man and nature, enlarging the human interest and adding to the appreciation of natural beauty; and for this reason sculpture in a garden is to be regarded not as an ornament but almost as a necessity, as like that last touch of colour in a picture which sets the whole canvas in a flame [29].

Statues of marble seldom look well in Italy, never in England, and of all discords none can be so jarring as to place among the flowers dreadful forms of disease and suffering, cripples or beggars, or the monstrous dwarfs that look down from the Valmarana garden[1] as if to symbolize the starved and stunted life of the wall-coping. Art, like laughter, should be the language of happiness, and those who suffer should be silent. Time and Care may wait without the gateway, but Time the ungracious guest, who is always late for the wedding feast and

[1] At Vicenza

early for the funeral—envious Time the spoiler of the roses, who lays his hateful scythe to the root of the fairest flowers, should have no image, no altar, in the garden, for it is by events and not by the measure of them that we grow old, and hours spent in a garden are stolen from Death and from Time. Only health and strength and beauty are at home among the flowers, shepherds and shepherdesses, youths and maidens in the garb of long ago, portly noblemen in periwigs and armour, warriors and Amazons, nymphs and satyrs, virtues and graces. We may personify the particular place in a figure or bust, taught by the gate at Capua and the pulpit at Ravello,[1] or commemorate an historic event by reference as in the cavalier's garden at Norton Conyers where a leaden warrior speaks discreetly of the Edgehill fight. We may represent the great elemental forces of nature, the higher motives which sway the human drama, the hoped-for triumph of Love over Death. We may build in some secluded nook a Cupid's altar, where many generations of

[1] The bust on the pulpit, formerly supposed to be a portrait of Sigelgaita the wife of the donor, is now held to be a representation of the city of Ravello. In classic times, cities were often represented by ideal figures, and the practice was revived in the thirteenth and again in the fifteenth century. Il Tribolo placed a bronze statue of a woman, representing the City of Florence, upon his fountain at Castello. At Villa Garzoni there are seventeenth century statues of Lucca and Florence

lovers shall carve their names and make their offerings of flowers, or may set in the four quarters of the garden our pageant of the Seasons: Spring, as a winged youth, primrose-crowned, with flute and flower-embroidered robe; proud Summer as a weary king; spendthrift Autumn with open purse and lifted cup and gathered fruit; hoary Winter having a sealed casket under his foot, his beard hung with icicles and his mantle broidered with double-faced jests. No statue, however bad, should be condemned to a desolate old age. In a decorative landscape the figures are never happy unless they are enjoying themselves, and in a portrait even ugliness is rendered charming by the presence of a child, a dog or bird. Diana in a garden should not be without her hound, nor Neptune without his sea-monster; Mars may be mated with Venus, Flora with Vertumnus, Cupid with Psyche; every Amazon should have her warrior and every nymph her satyr.

I have left almost to the last, the magic of water, an element which owing to its changefulness of form and mood and colour and to the vast range of its effects is ever the principal source of landscape beauty, and has like music a mysterious influence over the mind. It was, perhaps, of this that Wagner was thinking when he wrote that music is like a power of nature which men perceive but do not understand. In the sound of rushing or of falling water there is beauty of reflection, for it repeats and by repeating deepens the joy or sorrow of the listener's mood; but to those who hearken more intently water will speak with a voice of its own, a message of peace or strength or freedom, in the careless timeless ease of its flowing, the lulling monotony of rhythmic sound, the exhilaration of power. But its chief appeal is through the avenue of sight. Movement representing to the eye the essential character of living things,[1] the quality by which they reveal themselves, just as inanimate objects are recognized by form, a fountain or rivulet will be to the garden a well of living water. On the other hand, the reflections in still basins have a strangely restful effect. They are associated, as Ruskin points out [30], with the idea of quiet succession and continuance; that one day should be like another, one life the echo of another life, being a result of quietude, part of that great rhythm

[1] James, "Psychology," ii 173-4, 89. The eye cannot avoid following the movement of a waterfall, but continually recovers its position by a series of jerks. Exner has shown that the sensation of motion is distinct from that of colour in the human eye, where it has a special place in the lateral periphery of the retinal field, completely independent of the perception of objects. The faceted eyes of insects are specially adapted for the detection of movement. See Auguste Forel, "The Senses of Insects," 1908, p 8

of harmonious change through birth and death to birth again which is the heart-beat of the universe. In lake or pool or river, water emphasizes the prevailing note of the landscape, harmonizes the picture by distributing or echoing colours and forms, by "reviving" the tints of sky, foliage and flowers, and whether in movement or repose it fascinates the eye which returns to it again and again; it should therefore, both in park and garden, be found at the focus of beauty and interest. These water reflections are actually more delightful than the views they repeat [31], in the softness of the lights, the depth, transparency and intricacy of the shadows, the freshness and tenderness of the colouring, for the gloss of the water-film is like the coat of old varnish which mellows a picture; like the twilight it gives breadth, connection and unity; and the reversal of the image [32] by baffling perception makes the colours richer and the contrasts of light and shade more conspicuous. The effect goes even further than this. We have not merely an improved presentment but an altered composition. The landscape is repeated from a fresh point of view, that is to say from one as much below the surface of the water as the spectator is above it, and all the objects which make it up are seen under different lights and in different relative positions. It may thus happen that the foreground, instead of being merged in soft meadow or shadowy foliage, is silhouetted upon the sky; is relieved, as in Turner's drawing of Nottingham [33], not against the dark base of a hill but against its sunlit summit. The middle distance is cut out of the picture, there is a sharper gradation of values from the nearer to the more distant reflections, and the shadows are not merely a lower tone but spaces of an entirely different hue, to which the heightened power of reflection gives depth and variety. The blue of the sky is darkened and other colours are altered or omitted. If there is the least movement of the surface, vertical lines will be lengthened and rendered more emphatic, while horizontal lines will tend to disappear.

But the distant view in a water landscape can never be so beautiful as a simple rendering of reeds and foliage. The grandest effect of all is produced by formal canals, not too large, which reflect the pavilion at the further end and the lime avenues which hedge them in. For smaller pools, the first object must be to give the water-artist something to play with—richly carved balustrades as at Frascati with fountain masks of bearded river-gods that drop tiny runlets of crystal into the basin, or mossy crevices, or the golden bloom of lichened stone, or plants, if any such exist, whose leaves are dark above and light below. Baby faces may lean to meet the reflections or, as in D'Annunzio's novel, Love and Death may kiss each other. The larger or more vertical the angle at which one looks down, the greater is the difference between the scene and its echo [34]: we may thus, by slightly sinking the pool, reflect beauties of carving and surface invisible from above; phantom forms may reveal themselves, or sculptured figures in the water may be springing up to grasp the shadows. The effect may be complicated by strange effects of light admitted through a crevice between bank and balustrade.

In water the two pictures always contend, reflection and transparency being in inverse ratio to each other, and in some positions it may be better to abandon the surface and cultivate the beauties of the underworld. With a fountain basin, sculpture must necessarily be above the water, but in dealing with a still reservoir no such law is imposed upon us. We may have a merman's pool, fringed with floating lilies, where below the water-film are sea-maidens and gold-red fish and under-water palaces, and that strange power the eye has of clearing away reflections by the change to a longer focus will enhance the effect by a sudden thrill of surprise. Columns and opposing mirrors may give endless vistas of pillared halls, and if the pool is near the upper edge of a cliff a strange light may be thrown into it through an opening protected by glass. We may build up a dark screen of masonry behind it and illuminate it through a water passage from a pool beyond, or make the still more interesting experiment of "total internal reflection," [35] admitting the sun's rays in the late afternoon between the stems of a great hedge of beech or ilex at such an angle that the returning rays will lie along or actually under the surface of the water. Some of these will appear to be bizarre suggestions, and indeed it is likely enough that, except in great conservatories or winter gardens, under-water mirrors may produce an unquiet effect. But until such experiments have been tried, an opinion is of little value. There are no rules in art which some great artist has not shown us how to break with advantage, and every new adventure is a voyage of discovery, the outcome of which no man may foresee. Nature has "thousands of exquisite effects of light which are absolutely inexplicable," which can be believed only while they are seen, and by good fortune we may reap a larger harvest than we have sown.

Elsewhere the designer may prefer to play with the colour of water, seeking to reproduce those lovely hues of blue and green which the Italians of an earlier age caught and fixed in garden reservoirs, and even in small fountain basins. Water absorbs the red rays of the spectrum and is therefore a blue transparent medium, its colour when distilled being a tint of Prussian blue, as may be seen in the pure ice of the glacier crevasses. All that is necessary to bring out the natural beauty of the element by transmitted light is, firstly, a flood of strong sunshine; secondly, to look down from above as nearly vertically as possible; thirdly, to cut off reflections of the sky by trees or hedges or other dark objects. Suspended particles of glacier dust or chalk or lime add much to the brilliance of the effect, and in a country where the stone is red or yellow should give a tint of green or purple or violet. In England one may sometimes see blue or green pools at the bottom of a deserted stone-quarry: if experiment should show that good colour is unattainable at a higher level under these grey skies, we shall be justified in helping it out by the use of coloured tiles.

On the actual technics of garden-making volumes have been written, and I have no wish to add to the number. But there are still a few points which seem to have escaped attention. It should not be forgotten that there will always be one favourite or "set" view of house and garden. This may be worked up to, as an artist composes a picture, with water reflections and re-entering curves, studied masses of light and shade, the repetition of harmonious lines and forms, and especially with such a handling of scale, perspective, values and gradations of tone, as will enlarge rather than diminish the appearance of space and distance. With a new-built house, symbolic sculpture in the foreground may add the dignity of a larger meaning, and to an old hall that is yet unspoilt, broken fountain and weed-grown pavement may give the Pathos of Time. In addition to the "set" view, the route to be followed by visitors who are shown over the place should be considered as carefully as by Louis XIV at Versailles, a great part of the enjoyment of a garden lying in the power to give pleasure to others and to share the pleasure of one's friends.

One of d'Argenville's four maxims was always to make the ground look larger than it really is. This principle must not be carried too far. We should aim, as he tells us in another place, at that which is great and noble and studiously avoid the manner that is mean and pitiful, "not making little Cabinets and Mazes, Basins like Bowl-dishes and Alleys so narrow that two Persons can scarce go abreast in them; choosing rather to have but two or three things somewhat large, than a dozen small ones which are no more than very trifles." Yet undoubtedly a slight increase in the apparent size of the garden and, what is at least equally important, of the house, will add to the effect, and in any case we must be careful not to fall into the common fault of making them look smaller than they are. There are many little tricks of technique by which scale may be given. Every architect knows how converging lines, lowered steps and balustrades, slight successive reductions in the size and distance apart of statues, obelisks, vases, or other objects which repeat themselves, will lengthen the perspective. A curious illusion of spaciousness is produced in some of Knyff's engravings of old English gardens by a number of yew obelisks placed at equal intervals from each other. With a small and simple house and garden in a town, quite a good effect may be produced by a false scale, if the owner accepts it as a convention and is determined to be amused by the contradiction when giant figures come upon the scene. D'Argenville's maxim should be reversed when dealing with the approach to any building of importance, and the architect should follow the precedents of Hardwick, Caserta, and of that villa at Pratolino which was described as being "contemptible when seen from afar, but very fine when you come near it"; for as in the garden appearance should be greater than reality, so at the first view of the house expectation should be less than reality.

A principle which cannot be carried too far is Le Nôtre's law of contrast. It is not enough to consider this in the first rough scheme of the garden, in the general opposition of terraces to a great plain or of a broad flowery level to a landscape of rolling hills; we must apply it also at the boundary, where art and nature meet, and in every corner of the grounds, grouping together sunshine and shadow, grove and bowling-green, high and low, rich and simple, line and curve. In order to heighten the values of surfaces by contrast, every country house should have its paved court, its parterres of turf and gravel. The delicious softness of grass gives at the first footstep a release from care, which should be proffered close to the house, and if possible at a centre of beauty. Parterres of box and gravel have, independent of contrast, a peculiar dignity and beauty; it is not true, though often stated by English designers, that the Italians of the Renaissance would have preferred to use grass had the climate allowed. The colour and smooth surface of lemon-pots make a pleasant harmony with a box parterre, as stone vases and paving with a carpet of turf; indeed, in a green garden the walks should always be paved, the thin edge of grass upon gravel having a mean effect. In a long line of flower beds, rectangles should alternate with circles, tangled thickets of unrelated flowers with masses of the same flower in varied colours, so that there may be the added charm of unity in diversity. The best method of judging minor architectural features, such as piers and stairways, is to consider whether they are bold enough and quiet enough to take their place in a picture.

IV

TO MAKE A GREAT GARDEN, ONE MUST have a great idea or a great opportunity; a cypress causeway leading to a giant's castle, or a fountain cave where a ceaseless iris plays on a river falling through the roof, or a deep clear pool with an under-world fantasy of dragon-guarded treasure caves lit by unearthly light, or a mighty palace quadrangle lined with hanging gardens of arcaded terraces, or a great galleon in a lake whose decks are dropping with jasmine and myrtle, or a precipitous ravine with double bridges and a terrace on either hand. But it is possible to introduce a touch of imaginative beauty into almost any garden by finding the most perfect form for one of its features, or by giving expression to the soul of some particular flower or tree, as with the Virginian vine on the trellis arcades at Schwetzingen and the cypress in the Giusti avenue at Verona.

So, if it is to be a rose-garden, do not choose these stunted, unnatural, earth-loving strains,which have nothing of vigour and wildness in them, nor banish other flowers which may do homage to the beauty of a rose as courtiers to a queen. Let climbing roses drop in a veil from the terrace and smother with flower-spangled embroidery the garden walls, run riot over vaulted arcades, clamber up lofty obelisks of leaf-tangled trellis, twine themselves round the pillars of a rose-roofed temple, where little avalanches of sweetness shall rustle down at a touch and the dusty gold of the sunshine shall mingle with the summer snow of the flying petals. Let them leap in a great bow or fall in a creamy cataract to a foaming pool of flowers. In the midst of the garden set a statue of Venus with a great bloom trained to her hand, or of Flora, her cornucopia overflowing with white rosettes, or a tiny basin where leaden *amorini* seated upon the margin are fishing with trailing buds. If the place be away from the house and surrounded by forest trees, let there be a rose balloon weighed down by struggling cupids, or the hollow ribs and bellying curves of an old-world ship with ruddy sail and cordage flecked with ivory blossom, or one of those rose-castles which the French romance gave to the garden for a mimic siege in May, low towers of carpenter's work with flanking turrets and iron-studded postern. Such a *Château d'Amour* is represented on many a mediæval casket and mirror-case. Ponderous mangonels are bombarding the fortress with monstrous blossoms, while from the battlements fair ladies hurl down roses still heavy with morning dew full in the faces of the attacking knights [36].

Gardens consecrated to the worship of some particular flower have been in favour since the Ancient Sages devoted their old age to the culture of chrysanthemum or peony, but who has yet worked out the utmost beauty of blue iris or silver-chaliced water-lily, of sweet pea or pansy, or, sacred to the Queen of Heaven, the "flower and plant of light"? Who has realized to the full the glory of vine, or clematis, or honeysuckle, wistaria, or bougainvillae? If it be sculpture that you seek, try the effect of a fountain court of *amorini*, where baby loves are climbing the obelisks and the flower-vases, playing and splashing each other upon the water-edge, swimming out to a marble Nef whose mast and sail and homing bows are festooned with clambering cupids. Turn into marble Watteau's dream, "L'Embarquement pour l'Île de Cythère" or Fragonard's "Fontaine d'Amour." Let there be a childrens' corner, the Good Shepherd of the Catacombs with a lamb upon His shoulder standing amongst the little beds, or a Garden of the Happy Hours, where Time by the sun-dial is fast asleep, his hands and feet fettered with rose-wreaths, while on the steps below him the children are weaving their flower-garlands, wrestling, reading, singing, playing at war and art and marriage. If it be colour that you desire, let the view from the low parlour window be a flash of lavender-blue, centred with gold, remembering that wild Nature's loveliest effects are in this key of colour, as witness the hyacinths that repeat the sky, the purple tide of the heather, the Alpine anemones, the dark blue gentians of the Jura pastures; if a wall garden, throw round it a grey ring of castle walls, for in art it is only appearances that matter, and forgery is not a crime unless it fails to deceive.[1] Of historic motives for laying out there can never be a lack. The fruit trees and vine-covered trellisses that tempered the sunshine in the late Roman gardens, the pergolas and vaulted pavilions of the Normans in Sicily, the green tunnels of the fourteenth century, the stately arched hedges of Bacon's

[1] Near Pallanza on Lake Maggiore there is a strangely successful castle ruin built to protect a private garden from being overlooked from the windows of an hotel near by

essay, are well suited to any country where the summer heat is oppressive. How interesting to re-constitute a forgotten type, the garden of Queen Ultrogoth, the flower-orchard of the Dark Ages, the Paradise of William the Bad, the Gothic plea-saunce of Crescentius, of the "Roman de la Rose," of Chaucer, of the "King's Quair!" In every land there are countless old houses still disfigured by the bare lawn and tortuous ways of the landscape gar-dener, and no one will have lived in vain who is able to restore to one of them the melodious beauty of which Pope and Rousseau robbed it.

But we are not forced to confine ourselves to imaginative reproductions of the past. Invention was not exhausted in the eighteenth century when design went out of fashion. I know no reason why we should not have subtly curving terrace fronts and courts that sweep outward like the mouth of a trumpet to enlarge the view, and indeed but for the intrusion of the unhallowed *Giardino Inglese*, this might have been the natural development of the Rococo garden. How many flowery realms there are yet to conquer! Who has yet sought the summer coolness of a water labyrinth with rose-bordered canals, where a great pool serves for a lawn in front of the house and boats may pass among the fruit trees and the flowers; or the quaintness of a

garden of autumn fruit, where purple grapes hang
in jewelled clusters upon the wall, dwarf pears and
fairy apples are touched with quivering gold; where
gourds and pumpkins like strange reptiles have
crept out of the flower-beds to sun themselves upon
the pavers, some great as the wheels of Cinderella's
coach, some shaped by nature as punch-bowls or
urns or bottles or balloons or writhing serpents,
some moulded for sport into dragons' heads and
laughing masks and monstrous baroque faces? Who
has yet realized the poetry, the forlorn and elfish
beauty of a deserted garden? Who has worked out
the possibilities of a sea-shore demesne, or of an
amphitheatre in a quarried cliff, or—except at Syra-
cuse—of flowery paths that wind their way across
stony abysses? Who has made for himself the knots
and pergolas of a roof terrace where, as in Seneca's
day, orchards may be planted upon the highest
towers and whole forests may shake upon the tops
and turrets of the house? The false perspective
which Nero introduced about his Golden House,
giving across the lawns and lakes prospects of far-
off cities, might, if the limitations be frankly accept-
ed, be developed into a minor art, as indeed it is in
Japan. Flattened curves and contrasts of foliage are
often used to give the illusion of distance, and the
method can be carried further, for with flowering

shrubs one may represent a distant waterfall, or turn a commonplace hill, like that at Scarborough, into a snow-capped mountain.

But whatever the garden is to be, whether its roses are to clamber up the eaves of a cottage or the towers of a palace, this at least is necessary, that it should be made with a care for the future and a conviction of the importance of the task. According to Bacon, gardens are for refreshment; not for pleasure alone, nor even for happiness, but for the renewing rest that makes labour more fruitful, the unbending of a bow that it may shoot the stronger. In the ancient world it was ever the greatest of the emperors and the wisest of the philosophers that sought peace and rest in a garden. By the olive groves and flower-bordered canals of the *Academia* Plato discussed with his followers the supremacy of reason, the identity of truth and goodness. Among the roses and myrtles and covered walks of the Lyceum Aristotle taught that perfect happiness is to be found in contemplation, in the divine intuitions of reason. Theophrastus left to his pupils the shady theatre of their studies, and amidst the fruit and flowers Epicurus pondered how by wise conduct to attain happiness. In the garden of the Bamboo-Grove Buddha taught the conquest of self, and in the Garden of Sorrows a greater teacher was found, for we know that Jesus ofttimes resorted thither with His disciples. The cloistered paradises of Sicily and of the Arabs may have been made for fairer, frailer flowers, but the rose-tangled orchards of the Middle Age and the great gardens of the Renaissance did not serve for pleasure alone. In the romances we find the company playing chess in the apple-garden, singing, weaving garlands, dancing the carol, looking on at the play of jugglers, tumblers and dancing-girls, but here also they listen to the lay of the troubadour, and here part of the business of government is carried on. In the "Chanson de Roland," Charlemagne gives audience in a *verger* to the ambassadors of the Pagan King of Spain, seated on a golden chair of state beside a bush of eglantine under the shadow of a pine tree, and in "Garin le Loherain," Count Fremont, one of the great barons, receives a messenger sitting in a garden surrounded by his friends. Some of the great pleasure-grounds of the Renaissance were ever crowded with a great retinue of priests and lawyers, architects and painters, doctors and men of letters, to whom they offered change and rest and freedom. Others were the homes of a court, where laws were considered, finance was regulated, envoys were received; where in one arbour the Poet Laureate might be paying his addresses to the Muse, in another the

Treasurer be grappling with his budget, while by the fountain under the shadow of the cypresses the Prince and his companions were discussing the doctrines of Plato and the greatness of the ancient world. Many of the letters of René d'Anjou are dated from the garden at Aix, and a century later we find Queen Elizabeth giving audience in her garden at Hampton and one of her courtiers attesting a charter in his *viridarium* at Edzell. The garden, like beauty in landscape, is inimical to all evil passions [37]: it stands for efficiency, for patience in labour, for strength in adversity, for the power to forgive. Perhaps at the last, in contemplation of the recurring miracle of spring and of that eternal stream of life which is ever flowing before our eyes, we may find that it stands for something more—one of the three things the Greek philosopher thought it lawful to pray for, hope to the dying; for along the thread of time and consciousness the individual is never severed from the race; he is but a leaf on a tree, a blossom on a flowering plant; to the ocean of life he goes, and from the ocean he may return again. Gardens have coloured every dream of future life, every hope of happiness in this, and he who can make them more beautiful has helped to exalt the sentiment of religion, poetry and love. The older descriptions of Paradise are simple renderings of the pleasure-grounds of the Persians and the flower-orchards of the Dark Ages, imagination being able to picture to itself things more perfect than the eye ever saw, but not things diverse in kind [38]. The mind cannot anticipate an unknown sensation; the deaf mute cannot form an idea of sound, nor the man who is blind from birth have a mental vision. Every impression, whatever its elements may be, is an indivisible whole, differing from its parts and even from the sum of them as a chord in music from the notes of which it is composed, or a new flower from the plants that gave it birth [39], and it is thus always in the power of the artist to give us a fresh creation, something different in kind, as different as were the fountain courts of the Renaissance from the gardens of the Arabs, or the terraces of Helmsley from the alleys of Versailles.

St Carlo's unjust judgment on Cardinal Gambara —that the revenues laid out upon his villa would have been better employed in good works—has even now its defenders, and we have yet with us the "practical man" who, visiting the dream-gardens of Italy, can see nothing in the cypresses but bundles of faggots, in the flower-beds but baskets of vegetables, in the statues and fountains but heaps of road-metal, and goes away sorrowful at heart over the selfishness of these aristocrats, who waste on pride and luxury what might have been given to the poor. Yet in truth such a garden as that of Lante is a world-possession, and the builder of it like a great poet who has influenced the life of thousands, putting them in touch with the greatness of the past, lifting their thoughts and aspirations to a higher level, revealing to them the light of their own soul, opening their eyes to the beauty of the world. Architecture, the most unselfish of arts, belongs to the passer-by, and every old house and garden in which the ideal has been sought is a gift to the nation, to be enjoyed by future generations who will learn from it more of history and art and philosophy than may be found in books. Thus the garden-maker is striving not for himself alone but for those who are to come after, for the unborn children who shall play on the flowery lawns and chase each other through the alleys, filling their laps with treasure of never-fading roses, weaving amidst the flowers and the sunshine dream-garlands of golden years. They too will share the joys and sorrows of the garden, will learn to love even the humblest tribes of its inhabitants: the prodigal weeds that carry the banners of spring in procession upon the cornices, and the dwarf trees, dead to the world, that have rooted themselves like anchorites in the crevices; the tinted lichen which feed on pure air and sunshine and outlast the stubborn oaks, and the lowly mosses which drink in the dewdrops and the blue shadows of the mighty trees; the sweet-sighing herbs of the twilight; and the pale stars of earth which, stirred from their slumbers when night is dropping dew into the mouths of the thirsty flowers, call the out-cast moths to a honeyed banquet. They too will know bare winter's hidden hoard, when the earth under their feet is full of dreams—dim memories of misty morns and dewy eves, of the slumbrous warmth of the golden sunshine, the soft caresses of the life-giving breezes, the nuptial kisses of the bees. They too will feel the rhythmic breath of wakening life from the countless millions of beings in earth and air and dewdrop and rivulet, with the rising murmur of insect delight, the scent of the sun-kissed grasses—all the mystery and music, the riot and rapture of the spring, and the passion of the flaming roses, and that strange thrill of autumn sadness when the flowers that have mingled their perfumes through the summer are breathing out to each other the grief of a last farewell.

It is not given to every man, when his life's work is over, to grow old in a garden he has made, to lose in the ocean roll of the seasons little eddies of pain and sickness and weariness, to watch year after year green surging tides of spring and summer break at his feet in a foam of woodland flowers, and the garden like a faithful retainer growing grey in its master's service. But for him who may live to see it, there shall be a wilder beauty than any he has planned. Nature, like a shy wood-nymph, shall steal softly back on summer nights to the silent domain, shading with tenderest pencillings of brown and grey the ripened stone, scattering wood-violets in the grassy alleys and wreathing in vine and ivy the trellised arbour, painting with cloudy crusts of crumbly gold the long balustrades, inlaying the cornices with lines of emerald moss, planting little ferns within the fountain basin and tiny patches of green velvet upon the Sea-God's shoulder. As the years pass by and no rude hand disturbs the traces of her presence, Nature becomes more daring. Flower-spangled tapestries of woven tendrils fall from the terrace, strange fleecy mottlings of silver-grey and saffron and orange and greeny-gold make the wall a medley more beautiful than broidered hangings or than painted pictures, the niches are curtained with creepers, the pool is choked with water-plants, blossoming weeds are in every crevice, and with pendent crystals the roof of the grotto is fretted into an Arab vault.

Autumn has come at last, and the harvest is being gathered in. Flying shafts of silvery splendour fall upon the fountain, and all the house is dark, save for the strange light that is burning yet in the chamber window. Softly the Triton mourns, as if sobbing below his breath, alone in the moon-enchanted fairyland of a deserted garden.

REFERENCES IN THE TEXT

[1] "A New Voyage to Italy," ii 65 291
[2] G S Hillard, "Six Months in Italy" 1853
[3] "Modern Painters" 1898, v 218 (part ix chap i par iv)
[4] Forel, "The Senses of Insects" 1908, 3 122 196; Lubbock, "The Senses of Animals" 1889, 191–3
[5] W James, "Principles of Psychology" 1891, ii 298
[6] "Modern Painters" 1898, iii 140–1 (part iv chap x pars 8 9) 298–301 (part iv chap xvii pars 3–7)
[7] Ferrier, "The Functions of the Brain" 1876, 257–9
[8] Spencer, "Principles of Psychology" 1870, i 178 477 485 562 565–6 (pars 71 211 214 245 246); James, "Principles of Psychology" 1891, i 562
[9] "Modern Painters" 1898, iii 297–9 (iii xvii pars 2 3 4); James, "Psychology" i 558–9 254–5
[10] James, "Psychology," i 479 *note*
[11] Spencer, "Psychology," i 485 493–4 571 (pars 214 216 247)
[12] Spencer, "Psychology" 1870, i 191 258 (pars 76 116)
[13] Spencer, i 599–601 ii 593–4 (pars 261 519)
[14] James, ii 295
[15] Spencer, "Psychology" 1870, i 466 491 570; ii 580 (pars 208 216 247 514)
[16] James, "Psychology" ii 428
[17] Spencer, "Psychology" 1870, i 485 (par 214)
[18] "Modern Painters" ii 45–7 (part iii sec i chap v pars 6–8)
[19] "Modern Painters" 1897, i xl
[20] "Modern Painters" 1898, iii 310 (part iv chap xvii par 22)
[21] "Modern Painters" 1897, ii 34 (part iii sec i chap iv par 4)
[22] James, i 575
[23] James, ii 316; Grant Allen "Physiological Aesthetics" 1877, pp 175–80

109

[24] Ruskin, "Seven Lamps of Architecture," chap v

[25] Spencer, "Psychology," par 539

[26] See Sir Joshua Reynolds' Fourteenth Discourse

[27] Raymond, "Essentials of Aesthetics" 1907, 153–4; Ruskin, "Modern Painters" 1898, iii 141–8 (part iv chap x pars 9–18); W James, "Psychology" 1891, ii 124

[28] Bain, "Rhetoric" 1892, ii 29 53 206

[29] Ruskin, "Stones of Venice," vol iii chap i par 7

[30] "Turner's Harbours of England" 1856; note on the drawing of Scarborough

[31] "Modern Painters" 1897, i 345–55 (part ii sec v chap i pars 1–10)

[32] James, "Principles of Psychology," ii 81

[33] "Modern Painters" 1900, i 380 (part ii sec v chap iii par 8)

[34] Sir Montagu Pollock, "Light and Water"

[35] Sir Montagu Pollock, "Light and Water" 1903, 61 *note*

[36] J Westwood, "Description of the Fictile Ivories of S K Museum" 1883, pp 297 299 300 309

[37] Ruskin, "Modern Painters," iii 308 312 (part iv chap xvii pars 18 26–30)

[38] Spencer, "Psychology," par 187; James, "Psychology," ii 44; Ruskin, "Modern Painters," iii ii ii 10 and iv iii 23

[39] James, "Psychology," i 488 ii 2 *note* 30 45 270; Spencer, "Psychology" par 211

INDEX

INDEX

This book, *On the Making of Gardens,* by Sir
George Sitwell, BT, together with the *Introduction* by Sir Osbert Sitwell, BT, has been set
in 14-point *Bembo* type and printed on cream
wove paper hand made by Hodgkinson of
Wells in Somerset.
Of the two editions numbers 1-100 have been
bound in green Niger Morocco and numbers
101-1000 in green Buckram

Printed at the Dropmore Press
32 Great Ormond Street LONDON WCI
during September 1949